DA VINCI
VISITS
TODAY

AL LAUTENSLAGER

For permissions requests, please contact the
author at Al@AlLautenslager.com.

Front Cover Design and Interior Layout by
Cathi Stevenson and Gwen Gades

Contact the author via email at Al@AlLautenslager.com

Images: AdobeStock_182449681_ArTo
and AdobeStock_21089209_Mist

Print: 978-1-7350723-0-2

E-Book: 978-1-7350723-8-8

DA VINCI VISITS TODAY

Stay Curious!

Al Lautenslager

AL LAUTENSLAGER

Stay curious!

[signature]

DEDICATED TO
MAX SIMPSON

TABLE OF CONTENTS

PART I

PREFACE

"I love those who can smile in trouble, who can gather strength from distress, and grow brave by reflection. 'Tis the business of little minds to shrink, but they whose heart is firm, and whose conscience approves their conduct, will pursue their principles unto death."

-Leonardo da Vinci

The Dutch cabaret artist, Herman Finkers, implied that we make far too little use of the insights that already exist, the mistakes that have already been made, and the development principles already previously thought up. We have to learn from great people of the past. Who better to learn from, then and now, than one of the greatest thinkers of all time, Leonardo da Vinci?

You are about to do that.

If I told you Leonardo da Vinci just landed on our planet, in our country, in our city, would you believe me? Probably not, but it would make you immediately start to think that if he did, what would happen. What would he see? What would he say? What would you say to him? How would he measure up to the things that he was ahead of his time with, back in Renaissance times?

Oh, what we could learn. We could also see similarities, perspectives, comparisons, and observations from him that we take for granted today.

We could see his ways—how he almost planned for things—that have now come true, more than 500 years after his death, many of these helping to guide current thinking and future planning.

This book is part history and part futuristic. You've heard that history repeats itself. Nothing could be the case more than many of da Vinci's ideas, thinking, and lessons. Just listen to Mr. Finkers, as stated above.

I'll say it now, as it is said many times throughout: da Vinci was an artist, scientist, engineer, and architect among many other designated position titles. You are about to read more about how art was just one part of da Vinci's life, perspective, observations, and foresight.

This book takes you through an intellectual journey, in these capacities, as if he were by your side, along the way. Imagine having a conversation, a debate, a lesson from the master himself. If he visited today, you would be able to do this—unless he spent all his time observing, noting, sketching, and asking questions (which, as you will learn, he is famous for).

The purpose here is to stimulate new thinking about Leonardo and his ideas and lessons.

I know what you're thinking: not another Leonardo da Vinci book. Yes, but this one is different. It's okay to have another. After all, there are over 7,000 books written (so far) about Abraham Lincoln, close to 100 books about Elvis and over 2,000 books written about the Beatles. There are plenty of other da Vinci books written, but none with this approach.

That's why I'm not spending lots of time on his desire and interest in flying, his research into water, and his habit of dissection to grasp hold of the human anatomy. These are important, significant da Vinci contributions and notable, and are mentioned here, but will be left a bit on the side as da Vinci visits 500 years in the future.

Many have written and analyzed da Vinci's life with their own perspective based on their interests and areas of expertise. That's fine. *Da Vinci Visits Today* brings yet another, albeit new, perspective on all things da Vinci.

There are clearly two stories within this book. One is about the life and works of Leonardo, serving as a base for current observations. The other story is of his views of today, stepping into current times for the first time.

The goal is to stimulate your thinking, maybe develop new connections, new ideas, or even new theories, all through a book that will be an enjoyable read. This will appeal to the historians, the art aficionados, futurists, and entrepreneurs, for there are elements of interest for each, throughout.

Was Leonardo really a man with ideas before his time? Was he really that smart and rounded in his thinking? To answer these questions, we will embark on a journey that looks at everything he saw, heard, and sensed as if he were present, here, in current times.

This is not a biography. It is highly focused with a slant. Any one of these chapters or topics could be a book in and of itself. We have only touched the surface of each, given the context of *Da Vinci Visits Today*.

This book is based on a passion for history and Italy in general. My visits to that country, in particular Florence, Milan, and the Tuscany region, have fueled that even more and have propelled me to this point of sharing a perspective in this book. I have seen The Last Supper, many other da Vinci paintings in real life, and his memorial statue in Milan. All of that furthers my connection. I felt like I was around da Vinci the whole time I was there, in his country.

I intend to dig deep into Leonardo, certainly using the knowledge provided by the many researchers before me, but also from the perspective of Leonardo walking and living in the present day. There is a bit of conjecture here.

I am and have been an entrepreneur with a creative mind. Thinking like da Vinci is something I am proud of, and it has helped me along my entrepreneurial journey. His perspectives will arm you with methods and viewpoints to think like him. I even congratulate here Michael Gelb, who has published a book by the title, *How to Think Like Leonardo da Vinci.*

The points, within this book are thematic in nature, not necessarily chronological. There is a lot of historical background to set the stage for his mindset, perspective, and potential new connections. You will learn history. You will learn perspective. You will come away with a new way of thinking. That is the goal. That certainly happened to me during this writing. For all of this is a tribute from me and words of thanks to Leonardo. I feel connected. Hopefully you will, as well.

His visit and related observation could be monumental, to say the least. He would never be able to record all that he saw. He could never remember everything. He would not have enough notebooks or time to do what he was used to doing when coming upon new thoughts and ideas. That's the New World.

It is the hope, with this book, that you will now be able to see how complete a human being Leonardo da Vinci was, elevating him to a special status. He was a walking example of what one can achieve if passions are pursued and as imagination is combined with intellect. That achievement, many times, can evolve into new discoveries, new ideas, and new inventions, conceptually or real. Da Vinci was one who could achieve anything he set out to do.

Yes, you will see how da Vinci shaped history, then and now, all in addition to learning more about the world around you that you live in daily.

Giorgio Vasari, in his biography of Leonardo fifty years after da Vinci's death, stated, "Occasionally heaven sends us someone who is not only human but divine…"

In his time, Leonardo was appreciated by few of his contemporaries and many times had to fight for status. Compare that with today's time where he is revered, admired, honored, and appreciated by the masses.

Da Vinci's time was a time like our own. That is why we have much to learn from him, even 500+ years after his death. Now let's have the conversation with him. Let's go on his journey, with him.

The whole visit to another time, another world, would leave da Vinci with both foresight and reflection. Both contribute to future times. His reflection that we can all take to future times is offered by one of his own statements: "I love those who can smile in trouble, who can gather strength from distress, and grow brave by reflection. 'Tis the business of little minds to shrink, but they whose heart is firm, and whose conscience approves their conduct, will pursue their principles unto death."

INTRODUCTION

Mention da Vinci and many things come to mind. Certainly, the popularity, fame, and pop culture status of the movie, *The Da Vinci Code*, and the 2003 mystery thriller novel by Dan Brown created da Vinci awareness.

For the learned and well-read, da Vinci is associated with the Mona Lisa masterpiece painting and The Last Supper mural painting in Milan, Italy. But certainly there is much more, so much more that you have to wonder about his perspectives, visions, pathways, and goals to explain the unexplained, to solve the enigmas of life, and do it with style, grace, substance, fortitude, and the utmost authority.

Da Vinci was a painter, sculptor, architect, musician, mathematician, engineer, draftsman, military engineer, inventor, anatomist, geologist, cartographer, botanist, scientist, thinker, philosopher, a theatrical producer, writer—an overall visionary genius. Yes, all of those things and more.

With all of that, you cannot help but wonder what shape those perspectives and visions would take if da Vinci stepped foot on present day earth.

In order to understand that or to solve that historic conundrum, the inherent and superficial qualities of the man and his mind must be further examined. We must understand his true essence. Once examined, the grounded principles can be applied to any and all facets of the current, stepped-upon world, and into the future.

Leonardo da Vinci was known as the ultimate scientific genius. His artistry is second to none in his day, and perhaps even today. He has been labeled a technological wizard, among many other things.

Just look at what he is known for. His contributions are too numerous even to list here, completely, but one cannot ignore the significance and relevance of his scholarly body of work set in historical perspective, then added to future vision.

Consider just these few contributions and, for now, view them as influences to perspective—past, present, and/or future. Just imagine that at one time, these appeared on or were a result of Leonardo da Vinci's to-do list. He was responsible for:

- Creating artistic masterpieces: Mona Lisa, The Last Supper, Salvator Mundi,

The Vitruvian Man, St. John the Baptist, Lady with an Ermine, and many more

- Developing painting concepts (with new perspectives, techniques, and detail) of shadowing, use of landscapes, light, shadows, and perspective
- Proposing how the heart pumped blood
- Dissecting bodies/cadavers to study, understand, and document human anatomy
- Creating maps of entire uncharted sites
- Developing ideas for aggressive military machines
- Building theatrical sets and props for pageants, performances, and theatrical productions
- Inventing measuring devices
- Observing and studying birds and their flight
- Obsessing about human flight
- Diving into the subject of optics, including how light is processed by the human eye
- Studying the flow of water, erosion, and other geological phenomena
- Calculating proportions and

the relationship of every part of
the human body, proportionally
and mechanically speaking

♦ Performing and producing as
an architect, a master painter,
an engineer, and a sculptor

♦ Conceptualizing robots, military tanks,
parachutes, gliders, and helicopters

♦ Envisioning the city of tomorrow

Leonardo's life ranged across the perspective components of physiology, anatomy, hydraulics, engineering, invention, art, color, geometry, aeronautics, mechanics, acoustics, psychology, thought, and imagination.

There are more concepts, more studies, and more lessons, especially when diving deep into any one of the general topics and concepts. It literally would take an encyclopedia or staunch Google search listing to do justice to the full scope of da Vinci's accomplishments.

His influence lives on today.

If he had published his scientific thoughts, he would have had an even more massive influence on the development of science and mankind. Leonardo's approach to knowledge and methods set the stage for modern scientific thinking.

For now, we describe this, in order to gain his past perspective while laying the groundwork for future observations. It's also all described so as to share with you, someone with the mental capability of enormous perspective, analysis, solutions, visions, and curiosities in a time in the world when the foundation for the age of exploration and eventual European global domination was being laid; also known as the Renaissance period.

The Renaissance teaches that looking to the past for insights and inspiration can help in dealing with today's issues. History shows us that by looking to the past we can address current challenges that previous societies have faced, find potential solutions, and new ways of doing things.

One of the most fascinating periods in history is the Renaissance period, which covers the fourteenth and fifteenth centuries in Italy. The art, innovation, architecture, and ways of thinking during this time are astonishing and sometimes beyond belief, all the while capturing the imagination and interest of the Renaissance public. The Renaissance not only is a highly engaging period, but one that offers us lessons for life today and our many approaches to everyday living.

But why are we even talking about history? Why are we learning about past perspective? What can we learn that applies to today and even to future times?

Did da Vinci live in more interesting times? How did Renaissance culture stack up to today's modern culture? During the Renaissance, people looked to their past in search of a new direction. This is still true today, especially with a Renaissance visitor on site in present day.

ItalianRenaissance.org says it best:

"While the challenges that each generation faces differ from those faced by previous generations, many of the same basic concerns persist. How do we approach issues that we face today, whether they are related to society, living life or co-existing with all others of the world? Do we think that coming up with some new and progressive solution to problems is always the best, or do we stop and consider how similar problems were addressed at different times in history? By looking to the past for guidance today, not only can we find potential sources of answers, but also ways to address current challenges the way da Vinci did."

Leonardo has been studied since his time in the 15th century. Each study and interpretation finds him to be amazingly modern.

Let's consider Leonardo's meaning in our era. Our fundamental make-up as human beings has not changed since da Vinci's time, however the world around us, our environment, has changed at an astonishing rate, along with our perspectives on da Vinci's findings, thoughts, and accomplishments. This also continually changes our own perspectives.

Da Vinci and even others during Renaissance times showed us the importance of continual innovation and invention. Just look at what came out of that period, whether it be art, culture, inventions, or life values.

That's what made the Renaissance the age of exploration it was known for and later, an age of humanism.

Renaissance leaders were very forward-thinking in their approaches. This certainly included da Vinci but also included Raphael, Michelangelo, Brunelleschi, Botticelli, Verrocchio, and others.

Da Vinci's observations, perspectives, and logical analysis in areas of focus from astronomy to engineering, to anatomy and physiology, seem a far distance from anything his colleagues were doing. It took centuries (500+ years to date) for mainstream science to catch up with his insights. It's as if someone took a scientist from today's times and teleported him back into Renaissance times.

The Scientific Revolution was still in the future and not known by da Vinci during his time, except subliminally in his visionary thinking and applications. Da Vinci showed us time and time again how these new approaches were a way to address problems and come up with new ideas. Exploring principles of Renaissance perspective allowed for more innovation and exploration.

The Renaissance thrived by connecting the past, present, and future. The Renaissance period in Italy could be classified as being the best example of a time period with its feet in worlds of the past and in the future. Today, with his base of knowledge from the past, da Vinci would recognize how the past connected to the future.

ItalianRenaissance.org finishes by saying that the Renaissance was the "gateway" to the modern world. At least in some circles, it is called the "Early Modern" period—even if we might not ordinarily think of anything in the fifteenth century as being "modern" at all!

History makes us better decision makers.

What da Vinci had not yet realized was that he was truly a vessel of change. He had new ideas. He exemplified the Renaissance rebirth; he would be the catalyst and the innovator who would transform the world or at least his region of the world into an Age of Enlightenment from the Renaissance. Of course, this would happen after his time, but that transformation was all but logical given the direction, the events, the impetus, and ideas behind that path.

George Santayana (1863-1952), a philosopher, essayist, poet, and novelist stated, "Those that do not learn history are doomed to repeat it." His words hold true and are still very relevant today. History gives us all the opportunity to learn from the past, whether mistakes or successes. It helps us understand the many reasons that things happen and why people act the way they do. As a result, it helps us become more compassionate, well-rounded, and thoughtful as people, and better and smarter decision makers.

Explore those possibilities today, step into da Vinci's whole new world, and know that doing so will change who you are forever. Those possibilities were at the core of da Vinci's beliefs. He is about to prove (and live) those beliefs stepping into current times.

LEONARDO'S MISSION AND VISION

Leonardo had a passion for learning everything he could about the world he lived in and turning that knowledge into bigger and better things that would make life better for everyone. In this book, he is about to visit bigger and better things. He is about to see conveniences, entertainment, tools, and variety that make life better for everyone.

The artist in da Vinci wanted to make things better. The engineer in him wanted to make things better, faster, and more efficient. Da Vinci the architect wanted his work to be as much a product of his imagination as his painting. This all happens for us today, sometimes taken for granted and many times loved and enjoyed.

In addition, he always was imagining a world that was different than the one he lived in. Obviously, 500 years later, on the ground in a new city, that would be the case. He would wonder if it was the case below the surface (inner workings, basic concepts, people oriented, and any economies related). That's where his curiosity would stray as he experienced new things in new times.

URGENCY OF DOING THINGS

This could be said about da Vinci in his time and da Vinci during his visit to new times: Sure, da Vinci did a whole lot of observing. He did a whole lot of logging and sketching in his notebook and he did a whole lot of studying. Although not always written in his notebooks, he also spent lots of time asking questions, mostly, "what if" questions. He knew it was easy to get stuck in a mindset where thinking is substituted for action.

Da Vinci was a thinker as much as a doer. Giorgio Vasari stated in regard to da Vinci, "Men of genius sometimes accomplish most when they work the least, for they are thinking out inventions and forming in their minds the perfect idea that they subsequently express with their hands." That's da Vinci.

Leonardo, though, was more than just thinking and looking. He had a "doing" streak in all that he did—not always an immediate doing streak or even a consistent streak, but he did have a sense of accomplishment. Yes, he was a procrastinator, but look at what he did get done.

He did offer a tip on getting things done. Consider:

"It had long since come to my attention that people of accomplishment rarely sat back and let things happen to them. They went out and happened to things." People in new times could take an immediate lesson from this.

People can think and think and take action none of time, some of the time, or just once in a while. Da Vinci knew that to get things done, one has to do things. That's obvious. He also realized that there is no way to get around taking action if real life results are desired. He wanted results. He would want results from a visit to new times, not just an idle, sightseeing, suburban walk.

He went on to say, "I have been impressed with the urgency of doing. Knowing is not enough; we must apply. Being willing is not enough; we must do." If he was impressed by "doing" during his time, imagine the "urgency of doing" in all of the new hustle and bustle in view today.

PART II

STEPPING FOOT ON PRESENT DAY EARTH

The whole subject of time travel has been popularized for decades, mostly in philosophy and science fiction worlds.

While the books and stories of H.G. Wells, Jules Verne, and many more have stimulated the imagination of mankind and the relationship of the 4th dimension, the subject is still of a fictional and hypothetical nature.

The movie, *Back To The Future*, had humans travel to arrive at a point in time in the past and into the future. Time travel theories and hypotheses have been discussed, whether by Einstein, Steven Hawking, or by Marty McFly and Doc Brown, but mostly regarding traveling to the past.

This book is not about time travel as is talked about in science fiction, the movies, and philosophy circles. Time travel here is only a concept and mechanism to provide a means for observation, perspectives, comparison, and the furthering of historical application to today's world.

While da Vinci's philosophies, viewpoints, perspective, and visions can be discussed and expanded upon ad infinitum, let's look at the quest of what this incredible man with the multi-faceted mind would think about each part of life in today's world. Since he clearly was a man thinking way ahead of his time, let's look at him and review his thinking at a point way ahead of his time, as shared by him.

This represents movement and comparative thinking between certain points in time. It is not about the physical movement of a person with the use of a hypothetical device referred to as a time machine.

For now, we will leave time travel as that and make the literary assumption that somehow, some way, we are blessed with da Vinci's appearance and the ability to converse with him, today, in this sense: no machine, no abstract time-continuum theories, no physics… just an assumption to allow observation, conversation, thoughts, applications, and the study of his perspectives and of his overall essence.

PERSPECTIVE

This whole venture, for da Vinci, is an expedition in perspective.

Perspective is defined, by all of the major dictionaries, as a particular attitude toward or way of regarding something; a point of view. Perspective is the way you see something. This expedition is all about how da Vinci would see a new world in new times.

Perspective has a Latin root meaning "to look through" or "to perceive." All meanings of and references to perspective have something to do with "looking."

Changes in perspectives fuel curiosity. If there was one theme here, this would be it, unequivocally. Da Vinci had perspective then and he would now. He would be more curious than ever in looking around today and his perspective tank would be overflowing with that fuel.

Imagine da Vinci's perspective today. Who else to learn that perspective from than da Vinci, through his own eyes with his own thoughts.

THAT FIRST LOOK

At first, one thinks when approaching a new place (in this case for da Vinci, a future point in time in a future city), about what one will see: that first glance, first impression, first interaction, first set of senses touched, and more.

What is seen, felt, and sensed is framed from the past: experiences, knowledge, thought, mindsets, and one's psychological and environmental influences.

Leonardo was ahead of his time in many respects. That theme repeats throughout his lessons and accomplishments. This notion includes how he thought and observed; his insatiable pursuit of knowledge; his relentless curiosity. It's almost like all of this allowed him to see the future. His thoughts and perspectives suggested new possibilities. His imagination was not fogged by what would clutter and fog it today. His ideas really did emerge with futuristic thinking as an end-goal with a very grounded Renaissance base.

Pundits and experts have offered and identified those components employed by da Vinci that formed the base of his genius intelligence, in his quest for creativity and innovation amidst his curiosity of everything. These truly did enable him to view things differently, which led to different ways of thinking and different outcomes in his applications.

These qualities form the mind that, when stepping into new times, takes notice of new surroundings immediately. Taking notice leads to new thoughts, new questions, new curiosities, new and different applications, and more—just what da Vinci had in mind at every turn, every day, regardless of the time period.

Because he was a learned man of experimentation where he had to see something work or tested before he believed or understood it, he would want to duplicate much of what he ran across in his timely visit today. Not only would he want to reverse engineer it, he would want to engineer it. He didn't have time for that. Duplication was not needed. His thoughts would have continued on his Renaissance path where his studies, concepts, and inventions should serve to inspire. Today he could still inspire, putting duplication aside.

Leonardo, the artist, painted masterpieces. He was also a man of science, providing practical applications and solving problems, all with a logical approach.

Both the artist and the engineer were evident in his architectural drawings, notebook sketches, and more. Although he most often worked on castles, fortresses, churches, domes, and cathedrals, he also drew designs for buildings, bridges, streets, structures of all types, and complete, "visionary" cities.

His ideas and drawings gave ideas on the "working" of a building in addition to its outward physical appearance and sometimes beauty.

In looking at past drawings, one could see the similarities as he would see in present day buildings: doorways, windows, staircases, ornamentation, roof structure, and more architectural detail.

One vision Leonardo tried for in Renaissance times was an ideal city, built on several levels with connecting vertical staircases. Leonardo suggested the placement of stairs outside of buildings, primarily to give more space to the interiors of buildings. He also wanted to make various levels accessible from houses and other adjacent structures.

Looking around today, these building types would be present in abundance. Back in time, that vision of buildings was classified as unconventional. He was ahead of his time then, and his designs helped in shaping the building styles that he would lay eyes on in his visit to today.

Because of his mindset of always questioning the present, he often re-thought the design of buildings, streets, structures, and complete cities. He took their winding, overcrowded, narrow streets with houses, dwellings, and other buildings pressed against one another and developed something better, something different: a new cityscape. Imagine his list of "what-if" questions:

- What if buildings were spread out more?
- What if street patterns were on a very mechanical grid?
- What if there were no houses in the cityscape?
- What if there were no working areas in the cityscape?
- How could more parks and open spaces be built within a city?
- What if goods and services were traded in one concentrated area?
- What if all these different areas had unique architecture to identify them?
- Would it make sense to "stack" buildings?

It is peculiar that many of these questions would be answered with his current visit because they reflected Renaissance- era city characteristics.

His new thinking, and vision for that matter, consisted of a city with clean urban spaces, streets for the easy and efficient transport of people, goods, and general commerce. He also added other architecture to complement all this.

His visionary cities were considered modern, spacious, and well ordered. Many of Leonardo's views of the city, upon his arrival today would be eerily consistent with his future city visions developed in his time.

With a mix of the da Vinci touch, his unconventional, curious approaches, da Vinci first thought of a redesigned city as one with high, strong walls, with "towers and battlements of a necessary and pleasant beauty." His vision further contained, "the sublimity and magnificence of a holy temple," along with, "the convenient composition of private homes."

Would da Vinci's view of today's city satisfy and be consistent with his visions? Would it satisfy his curiosities? Yes, curiosities would be satisfied except for the fact that his curiosity about anything and everything was clearly un-ending. He included within his past designs and probably in his current observations:

- Well-designed, stylish palaces
- Wider streets
- Walking leisurely and unobstructed pedestrian flow
- Services, trade, and commerce flow away from sight, out of the way of people, while highly functioning

This design is familiar to Renaissance times and that feeling of familiarity would partially be there for da Vinci, when observing today.

MORE ABOUT THAT FIRST STEP

More than 500 years have passed since Leonardo's passing. Many of his thoughts on city design wouldn't fit in today's world, but many of his related ideas are still considered, used, and applied today and for cities in the future. Ideas include concepts of verticality of living and working spaces, the need for life's essentials—food and water, along with open spaces and the pursuit of nature, just part of what would be considered and observed when da Vinci visits today.

So, what does he see, new to his eyes and familiar to his thoughts and experiences? Imagine a blink of an eye, a snapshot of an observation, over and over in movie-like fashion, frame by frame. Imagine recording those moments and re-watching them.

Today, he would see and sense:

- Streets with divided traffic flow
- People everywhere: coming, going, working, playing, and living
- Family units, pleasure seeking, sports or otherwise, and everyday living
- Pedestrian walkways and gathering areas
- Signs, advertising, videos, and

sounds to go with all that

♦ Buildings of different shapes, sizes, orientations, interiors, and exteriors

♦ People movers: cars, watercraft, mass transit, and flying machines of all shapes, sizes, and colors

♦ Smells of foods, preparation of food, packaging and delivery of food, variety of foods

♦ Modernization and automation

♦ Nature, nature, and more nature

These observed "elements" were best described by da Vinci himself and still hold true today, when he stated that, "The earth is not in the centre of the Sun's orbit nor at the centre of the universe, but in the center of its companion elements and united with them."

Companion elements are all there is. All of what he would see are companion elements.

Was this the precursor to his future city vision?

Da Vinci's vision here has dramatic parallel to his famous prophecy regarding water flow and the flow of rivers:

"In rivers, the water that you touch is the last of what has passed and the first of that which comes."

In this, he refers to time and its effect. We are all affected by time in all directions: The past pushes us from one side to another, the future pulls on us and we exist in that flow in the present moment.

Landing, viewing, and immediately observing are affected by these da Vinci thoughts and perspectives and that city in present flow.

Roman cities had a hierarchy of streets, effective patterns for their own traffic flow, in their case, pedestrians, crowds and mobs, and chariot flow. These patterns are part of every city today. All cities follow a pattern, whether a well-organized "metropolis-like" city or a chaotic town. The pattern of a city is the way different functions and elements of the settlement form and how they are distributed and mixed together in all dimensions. These patterns all encompass layout, architecture, space planning, transportation, pedestrian flow, services, culture and customs, and even the attitudes, whims, and notions of its people.

Every city follows a pattern. Da Vinci would immediately observe patterns.

Da Vinci would certainly observe the elements as well. He did this when devising his ideal city and he would do it in present day.

Da Vinci would take one look and notice the number of buildings, the various sizes, functionality, designs and more. He would even encounter buildings being constructed. Back in his times, construction was not an easy thing even though many constructed marvels were produced. The ability to do the things taken for granted today of moving and lifting were seriously limited. Mostly one would see horses and oxen carrying different materials from source to job location. What da Vinci immediately surmised was the simple excavation and hauling equipment, in new times, could easily do the work equal to hundreds of men in his time. Construction was a whole new area of interest and one he would be very curious about, especially with all the mechanical movement, architecture, and production. He would have the urge to sketch out the mechanical side of the equipment observed.

He would see people that obviously were not on their farms, at their homes or working for others, or at least that was what it appeared to be. Vehicles (not known by that name) moved in all directions on the hard, flat surfaces called streets and avenues, not strada or via as he knew the Florentine and Milanese alleyways to be. He would see lots of people almost simultaneously speaking to one another on square hand-held boxes/devices.

He would definitely be asking of himself or others around how something was lit without candles, lamps, or oils. Why wasn't there any smoke? Where were the fireplaces? What was used to keep the rooms at a livable and most comfortable temperature? He would see no farmyards, cattle or horse quarters (he was in the city).

No fortresses or walls were in place for attacking armies. Threat seemed to be absent. It would appear peaceful.

Da Vinci would land in a city. The city doesn't matter. How he got there didn't matter. His sense of time would be almost non-existent. Would he deem this an experiment?

He would observe those at desktops, not sketching, not even writing, but pressing keys on a device that would transfer thought and words to paper or behind the screen of this device, only to be brought back instantly at any time. Was this part of everyday life?

The whole concept of electricity had yet to be invented in Renaissance times so da Vinci would question things like wires, lights, and power and how all this worked together for devices, machines, automation, and more. Where did the power come from? How did it get there? How is it replenished? Is it safe? Does it cost anything? What kind of manpower is required? How could this be connected to something else for new and better ideas?

The lights adorning the buildings, and many other things besides, are fed not by what he knew as naphtha fluid but by something else, a second component, invisible to the eye, that can be conducted along metal wires, coated in a strange material. (According to New World Encyclopedia, Naphtha is a name given to several mixtures of liquid hydrocarbons that are extremely volatile and flammable. Each such mixture is obtained during the distillation of petroleum or coal tar.) By means of this component, ovens can be heated without the need for wood or other fuel, and stairways and metal boxes can be made to move, to convey people within buildings. This component can also cause the sound of a lute, or other instrument, or many instruments, to be greatly increased, so that its music could be heard even by a great multitude gathered together. Da Vinci is now in a land of variety and enhancements. Welcome to new times in the New World.

Light as it was known and used in the modern world, would be a whole new dynamic for da Vinci.

Whether a daytime visit or certainly a night time visit, lights would be dominant in the New World view. Taken for granted today and operated by the flip of a switch, da Vinci would ponder lit globes and wonder where the light came from, how they would go on and off with the flip of a switch, how they could give a steady glow/supply of light. Where were the candles? What about oil for candles?

In very limited spaces would he witness the candles he was used to, the glow or the smell, but he wouldn't take his eyes off of the globes and tubes full of candlelight.

Da Vinci was used to lighting for his pageants and theatrical events, even before he studied shadows for painting. Lighting at the beginning of the Renaissance in Italy consisted of three types.

The first, and most common light source, was the flaming torch. The second type was an oil lamp as we know it today, made of ceramics or metal. A wick was used for the burning of animal or vegetable oil. The third type was a candle, popular and mass produced since the 15th century. The sources of light in the New World would seem almost unending, whether for buildings, outdoors, signage, vehicles, and more. Imagine a trip 500 years back without a light switch to flip for light. That was da Vinci's new perspective comparison.

Da Vinci, at this point would be experiencing major overwhelm. Many times, during his observances, he would have to stop just to collect those overwhelming thoughts. Collecting, recording, sorting, and prioritizing became his new world, new times, modus operandi.

Plain and simple, da Vinci would experience major sensory overload whether in the form of information, technology, or surroundings. Envision it. He walks into a world with medical solutions and procedures, more choices and volumes of food and nutrition all leading to greater comfort for all. Local food stores, grocery stores, and restaurants would afford way more food choices and drink, much like that for the royalty of Europe. In fact, for da Vinci, the food might be more surprising and take a lot to get used to, as much as the technological influences.

Da Vinci was a scientist and separate from the rest of the scientific pack of his time. That meant that his knowledge, hypotheses, and observations were head and shoulders above the rest. Science in modern times would be at even higher levels, mind boggling in the least, at least to da Vinci. The wealth of new art and entertainment would be at an amazing level. Modern plumbing would be a whole new astonishment. Add to that running water, hot and cold, and the disposal of it after use, and da Vinci's engineering mind and inquisitive nature would go wild. Da Vinci would see many people doing a variety of things, hopefully by their choice, pursuing lives that they wanted. That would make him very satisfied as he tried to provide the same opportunities during his times, in his cities.

Da Vinci might see some similarities related to art, architecture, building, and the like but he would see many more differences. Fortunately, he was the right traveler to this time as he, among other Renaissance participants, was accustomed to the idea of change just like it was happening in their rebirth, right before their eyes, in 15th century Renaissance times.

Stepping foot in new times would not change his many current interests, curiosities, and talents. What would change would be the topics of interest and pursuit. Instead of the fundamentals that he excelled in—engineering, art, science, botany, anatomy, and more, his interests and pursuits would change to more modern topics and focuses. He would be observing and learning about computer science and information technology, graphic design, programming, advanced mathematics, industrial design and management science, more mechanical engineering, artificial intelligence, medical studies galore, photography, and health science. His mindset would be to study, break each subject down into detailed components to understand its inner workings, and then use all that to connect and create something new, maybe even bigger and better, helping more people. He would draw on other work and research to incorporate into newer designs addressing problems that were just waiting for solutions.

This would beg the whole topic of reverse engineering. Leonardo wouldn't know it by that term but he surely would understand the concept and context.

He would have a strong desire to take any man-made object and deconstruct it to reveal its designs, workings, and architecture, all the while extracting knowledge from the object being deconstructed. His approach to reverse engineering would be very similar to his scientific research of natural phenomenon.

Da Vinci would need to be careful of dwelling on conceptual work as new times were very results-oriented, reaching results at a much quicker pace than he would be used to.

The initial parts of his visit, 500 years later, would reveal more: how da Vinci would love to be involved in anything technological, especially if it was on the cutting edge. He loved to tinker but he wouldn't know what was cutting edge and what wasn't. Anything here, in new times, compared to his times, would be considered cutting edge.

Da Vinci would love movieland and television production. For much of his career, da Vinci was involved with designing dramatic sets for plays and stage productions. Da Vinci would want to immerse himself in theatrical production involving flowing gowns, pageant costuming, elegant dance performances, and his version of special effects.

For da Vinci, this visit to present times is just over 500 years after his death. Just half that time ago, people would have challenges comprehending even some of the simple things of today. People from da Vinci's time, except for da Vinci, probably, would view those in new times as having super, god-like powers, as witches or magicians. Da Vinci would take it more as a matter of course.

A DAY IN THE LIFE

Imagine visiting somewhere 500 years after your death. That's what da Vinci is doing. People in his time and now would go about their everyday business in one of many fashions. Just what was that day in the life like? How different would it be to yesteryear? The differences would be immense to say the least. Da Vinci would see these immediately but reconcile that with his daily life and what he was familiar with.

On any given day, he might choose to spend his time or parts of his day, drawing, or in front of an easel painting or tinkering, sketching and thinking about his various scientific ideas, surely bouncing from interest to interest, mostly on unscheduled whims.

There would, however, be a very good chance that he spent time socializing with his noble patron friends and their friends and associates, as well. For it was this socialization and friendship that gained him support, patronage, and work for the many parties and celebrations they were involved with. Producing celebrations, pageants, and dramatizations were all forms of his early employment to garner a livable wage.

Da Vinci would be quick to recognize, while trying to decipher the lifestyles of the bustling public, that those lifestyles were as varied as the individuals he observed. This was certainly true in the city of Florence as well as the rural areas surrounding the city, back then. He would observe differences between rich and poor, elite and labor classes, and city workers and farmers. Today, he would see differences between professionals and students, family people and single people, hard core business professionals and casual free-lancers.

One first thought, when viewing the masses of people among the hustle and bustle, was why the people were not peasant farmers working right now on the farm, raising crops. Today's people worked long and hard days. Peasants and others of Renaissance times worked hard days, too, but were sure to have religious feast days off in abundance. Farming work was seasonal, allowing for off season time for socialization, family time, talking, and entertaining each other. Would that be the case today with so few farmers in the midst? How were religious holidays and feast days treated? More observations lead to more questions.

Women of da Vinci's time spent their day's activities much differently than most men. Children, of course, spent their time and day's activity differently as well. All lifestyles observed would be different.

When da Vinci walked the city streets and piazzas in Florence, he was among monks, craftsmen, city ambassadors, artisans, nobles, and shop merchants. He heard lots of talk, back and forth, the bartering and conversation of textile buyers and sellers in shops filled with goods, rich fabrics, and other crafts. In the Florentine artists' workshops, he truly saw the splendor and beauty of Florentine art.

In order for da Vinci to understand daily life in the Renaissance, even though he lived it, he would have to examine the customs of various peoples during the early and late Renaissance, and examine the social, political, cultural, and economic factors that affected people's everyday lives. The same factors influence daily life today, which he would want to understand as well.

Gender and societal class also shaped daily life. Da Vinci knew this and was used to seeing upper-class women mostly in the home. They usually went, when accompanied, to the market, to visit merchants, to visit the church, or observe or participate in civic, city, or religious events. They also educated their children. Middle-class women were typically artisans crafting their crafts or shopkeepers for the trade, while those women less fortunate worked the fields, on the farms, or as servants in the homes of the elite. Noblemen were involved in notary (legal) activities, at war, or involved with the management of land and estates.

Leonardo would step into the New World and see that a day in the life centered around being consumed by electronic devices, phones, computers, televisions, technology of any and all kinds, video, work/jobs/ employment, service, and all the activity to make this happen at home and away.

Da Vinci would observe that this lifestyle led to a situation where there was not much time left for thinking, solitude, quiet, and leisure, as he would define it. He would ask, "…is a busy life a successful and productive life?"

Since da Vinci's original upbringing was studying art, he would always have an artistic influence in all that he did, even in daily life.

Once da Vinci started to figure things out, he would start to think of himself more a part of this world. He would definitely be involved in engineering for a company and/or eventually work towards an entrepreneurial venture utilizing his talents while providing him the means for sustenance. He would pursue his interests as hobbies, as well, and probably tinker in the areas of video production, graphic design, and art in one fashion or another.

For da Vinci, most of his time was spent working, investigating, and studying the things around him. Even in his early years, his prime, and his waning years, he always felt and lived as if there were not enough hours in a day to pursue the interests and curiosities in front of him. Things like sleep just got in his way. Even though he knew it necessary, he didn't sleep much.

Da Vinci had a strange sleeping routine. He never

viewed a day as the awake period between two long sleeps. His waking periods between short periods of sleep were like many resets to the whole day. Resets keep the mind fresh, which da Vinci was all about.

Da Vinci's sleeping habits and patterns meant that he never really reached an end to a day. He refreshed during short sleeps but never did one long reset.

He might be surprised to find out that sleep research of today cites the optimal sleep cycle as one 7-8 hour long period. It's a wonder how his sleep division would help him maintain his food regiment, his mental faculties, and health, and his overall immune system to fend off ill health, but he would not like the end of a day followed by a long rest.

Combining his unusual sleep patterns and habits along with his daily life routines would continue to keep his productivity at a high level.

Da Vinci viewed, in the course of a new day, people hustling and bustling, coming and going, playing and working. Work, in da Vinci's mind, immediately conjured the thought of things like work-life balance. He never called it that and really didn't need the balance that we think of today, but his balance was moving from one project or activity to another over and over; albeit one incomplete project to another incompletion.

A quick comparison of life during da Vinci's time and current times daily routine:

Daily Routine Comparison

	THEN	NOW
Sleep	Sleep—20 minutes every 4 hours	8 hours on, 16 off
Eating	Eating—as food was available; sustenance	Breakfast, lunch, dinner—planned menus or out to restaurants
Journaling	Notebooks galore, charcoal pencils, paper, bound	Blogs, online notes
Self Reflection	Within notes	Holiday/vacation time
Physical Activity	Not much but attention paid to health	Health clubs, yoga, personal trainers, weight lifting
Thinking/ Doing	Experimentation, observing	More accelerated
Physical Labor	As needed	As needed but much less
Social	Friends, work associates, officials and mentors	Online, networking, dinners, social media
Working/ Making a Living	Commissions	Salaried jobs, free-lance assignments paid by companies and owners, very little commissioning
Travel	Horseback/ mule/walking	Planes, trains, automobiles, buses
Leisure	Some	Sports, hobbies, experience based; life balance

NOTEBOOKS

All of this observing, watching, looking, and studying would give da Vinci an impulsive reaction to reach for one of his notebooks. He wrote down notes during Renaissance times and he would write them down now, in current times. He would sketch, draw, analyze, and record all of the world he encountered. Anything life-related would be observed, questioned, recorded, thought about over and over and over and maybe even re-sketched and re-noted.

The da Vinci notebooks would live on.

Leonardo carried a notebook with him at all times, encased in fine Italian leather and often attached to his belt or garb of the day. He had it at the ready so he could grab the notebook at the opportune time, or when something caught his eye, to record ideas, thoughts, impressions, and observations as they occurred. In the course of his everyday life, he would observe, think, switch areas of interest, but invariably stop along the way, many times, to note his thoughts, to sketch out ideas, to make his lists, to draw and more, in one of his many notebooks.

His curiosity was never-ending. He wanted to know everything about everything, whether practical or not. That was his wish. That was his vision and that was his mission in all that he did.

His notebook entries consisted of lists, sketches, and lots of detail-oriented notes.

Take, for example, the notebook entry* detailing his approach and outcome to his plan of mapping out and drawing the city of Milan (notice a few distractive thoughts along the way, even in his own list making):

- ◆ Calculate the measurement of Milan and suburbs

- ◆ Find a book that treats of Milan and its churches, which is to be had at the stationer's on the way to Cordusio

- ◆ Discover the measurement of Corte Vecchio (the courtyard in the duke's palace)

- ◆ Discover the measurement of the Castello (the duke's palace itself)

- ◆ Get the master of arithmetic to show you how to square a triangle

- ◆ Get Messer Fazio (a professor of medicine and law in Pavia) to show you about proportion

- ◆ Get the Brera Friar (at the Benedictine Monastery to Milan) to show you De Ponderibus (a medieval text on mechanics)

- ◆ Talk to Giannino, the Bombardier, re. the means by which the tower of Ferrara is walled without loopholes (no one really knows what da Vinci meant by this)

- Ask Benedetto Potinari (a Florentine merchant) by what means they go on the ice in Flanders

- Draw Milan…

- Ask Maestro Antonio how mortars are positioned on bastions by day or night.

- Examine the Crossbow of Mastro Giannetto

- Find a master of hydraulics and get him to tell you how to repair a lock, canal, and mill in the Lombard manner

- Ask about the measurement of the sun promised me by Maestro Giovanni Francese

- Try to get Violone (the medieval author of a text on optics), which is in the Library at Pavia, which deals with the mathematics

(As detailed in the book by Toby Lester Da Vinci's Ghost: Genius, Obsession, and How Leonardo Created the World in His Own Image (Free Press, 2012)

Leonardo believed that he had to dedicate a certain portion of his day focused on a single topic without the distractions of other topics, other people, or other environmental influences. He had to do this, sometimes for several hours at a time in a day's time, depending on his project or topic of interest at the time. In all reality, sometimes he did this and sometimes he just couldn't. His interests and curiosities were just too varied and too voluminous. Today's fast-paced world would not afford the thinking time he would be used to or want, especially with everything new that he observed.

Leonardo da Vinci, however, did master his balance of time and priorities more than people give him credit for, as he was able to paint masterpieces while spending parts of his days developing inventions and innovative solutions for everyday Renaissance opportunities or problems.

Thanks to the patronage of those in support of Renaissance artists, Renaissance-era writers, artists, innovators, and thinkers were able to spend their days doing just the art, the writing, the innovation, and the studying behind all that they did. This was the humanistic approach, popular and growing during Renaissance times. In this way, artists didn't have to "worry" about being employed in ordinary jobs or tied to the monastery. The artisans of the time could enjoy their daily lives traveling all around, studying ancient ruins, researching Greek and Roman philosophy and writings, and observing daily phenomena and topics of interest, much like da Vinci did, all at their own pace, a comfortable pace (for them).

Leonardo was surely a lover of the world around him. He was inspired, stimulated, and motivated to learn more.

Da Vinci's notebook thoughts followed his mind. They wandered. They were all over the place with no real organization. A note was made when thought occurred. Call him a free spirit with a free mind with sporadic focuses. Going about his day with this mindset would be what a day in the life would be like for Leonardo da Vinci.

THE IDEAL CITY

Da Vinci must have known he may someday visit the future.

He designed the city of the future, 500 years ahead of its time. Leonardo was influenced by the vibrancy of Florence. This influence helped shape his viewpoint as well as his ideas for the future. They would surely shape his perspectives landing in the city of his journey today. Five hundred years from da Vinci's time brings us to today, so his design was what he thought the city would look like if he landed here today. That premonition was real.

Da Vinci called it optimized, but how did he know what optimal conditions really were? If we define optimal conditions of a city today, would they look the same as his optimal thoughts?

He called his optimal space clean and urban. Did he even know what urban meant? He probably didn't use that specific word as the word urban was conceived in the 17th century, way after da Vinci's time. Urban means "of a city," so da Vinci was clearly designing his city of the future with the same meaning, just not the same word.

If Leonardo da Vinci were to witness today's megacities, he'd be appalled and frustrated by things like overpopulation, waste, and clutter. He would see that overpopulation had reached a level where natural resources were threatened and disposal of waste was a huge problem.

Even though he had created and planned an ideal city he would still be frustrated; his plans must not have been followed completely. He thought his urban development was rational at the time and it still could be rational. His model was one of harmony and an organized city.

One item of note about da Vinci's urban planning, was that it was done during a time when a plague hit the city of Milan. He was commissioned to study the causes leading to the conditions of the city as a result of the plague. He realized that crowded medieval city conditions caused the onset of disease and contributed to its rapid spread. With everyone close together, disease would spread rampantly. Waste built up and people did not like being that close to one another and let each other know about it.

During that time, cities, buildings, and houses that were close together led to problems. Coming up with solutions for these problems was something da Vinci thought about in his ideal city design. That proverbial light bulb went off and da Vinci had ideas for solutions to solve these issues and more.

His new city design considered:

- Roof shape
- Window configuration
- The use of glass as available
- The different building material choices
- The look, appearance, and style of the many buildings
- How things worked; people flow
- Doorways, arches, ornamentation
- Comfort
- Security
- Living space and home environment
- Business in a building

You could almost take this same list and apply it to city design of today.

The filth, waste, the civil unrest, the smell, the crowded space, and streets all led Leonardo to imagine an ideal city, based on efficiency, cleanliness, and things like a rational distribution of space and people. It was a city that promoted efficiency and increased livability for residents.

Da Vinci was a solutions provider with his thinking, observations, and eventual applications. His engineering side provided perspective and solutions that would make things faster, more efficient, and more pleasing to mankind. His emphasis on art and his architect's eye aided him in designing cities, buildings, and more to make living spaces better, more pleasing, and functional. He did this by combining theory, experience, and practice on both sides. As a side note and in support of those three components, setting foot in today's time, he would be impressed and an avid supporter of universities, think tanks, and anyone involved with applied sciences: those highly involved with combining theory and practice; those involved with theoretical and practical urban planning.

He observed these things then and he would do the same now.

Da Vinci had the well-being of the citizens of a city in mind. He wanted the best services, disease prevention, space, efficiencies, and more for the citizens of this hypothetical city. Looking around today he would see, maybe not clearly at first, everything around him with the citizens in mind: service establishments, efficient roadways, open recreational space, clean and organized living quarters, pedestrian flow, trade and retail businesses, and more.

Many questioned the organization of Renaissance cities after the Plague that killed about one-third of Europe's population happened during the 15th century. Redesigning layouts and solving problems of cleanliness, disease prevention, and transport were the keys to new urban planning. Da Vinci, peering out at today's city, would see attempts at cleanliness. Clean cities minimize the spread of plagues and diseases. He would observe public litter baskets, landfills, recycling facilities, trash bins on sidewalks, and effective trash collection in homes. Da Vinci knew this way of urban planning and the benefits it brought in preventing disease, before the days of scientific testing and true medical research.

He would observe efficient traffic and pedestrian flows, squares, walkways, plazas, and open environment areas as part of the ideal city solution. Urban planner then and urban planner now.

Da Vinci's ideal city was never built, however his recordings, notebooks, and codices containing his forgotten ideas surfaced many decades later to bring about much of today's urban planning.

Today he would see river walks lined with shops and establishments, downtown main streets, recreational lakes and rivers, along with many functional and ornamental fountains.

A water distribution network was on da Vinci's mind, thanks to the invention of hydraulic machines that could be placed in various rooms of buildings. His urban planning included the use of hydraulics, staircases, principles of verticality and more.

Water, the flow, the appearance, and characteristics were part of his urban planning. These characteristics are in clear view today. Da Vinci's hydraulic engineering orientation, along with his interest and study of all things water-related, could fill volumes. In fact, his notebooks reveal that the study of water and water dynamics was one of his most regularly studied topics.

Aside from water as being part of an ideal city, da Vinci studied pedestrian flow and commercial transport. He always had visions to improve these. He knew then that alleviating crowded streets prevented clutter, poor hygiene, and the spread of disease. Functionality, in his case, consisted of creating that clean, organized city alleviating overcrowding, waste, and disease, while pleasing citizens of the city. Many think, and da Vinci would observe, even in today's time, that cities built upwards not outwards, integrated with water systems and other nature with an efficient transport infrastructure, would be ideal. This would be the key to sustainability, efficiency, and general convenience for those within it.

Putting art and past perspective aside though, he would view the city of today as a concrete jungle, as Webster defines it, a modern city or urban area filled with large buildings full of concrete and windows, and regarded especially as an aggressively competitive, unwelcoming, or dangerous/ hazardous place.

He wouldn't be happy being unable to see the stars at night as tall buildings blocked his view or distracted his observation. He wouldn't be happy with the many advertisements speckled amongst that jungle and buildings. He would view this as a detraction of nature and question their being, purpose, and aesthetics.

Just a quick note on advertising during the Renaissance period of time as reported by Sergio Porrini, *ItaliaLiving.com* contributor:

A Fifteenth century fresco is probably one of the first advertising examples in history. Most marketing experts would say this reporting is a stretch, but it does present a Renaissance perspective that is underlying in da Vinci's thoughts and descriptions.

The famous Benozzo Gozzoli's frescos are located in the Magi Chapel at Palazzo Medici Riccardi. These frescoes were produced under commission by Piero de' Medici, Lorenzo the Magnificent's father. Beyond the religious meaning of the *Procession of the Magi*, a clear political message is given. The Medici were the rulers of Florence, and the characters shown in the frescoes are actually friends and allies of the Medici family. That's why these frescoes are probably one of the first examples of *advertising* in an era—the Renaissance—when television, newspapers, magazines and the Internet were not available yet!

Earlier, it was stated that every city follows a pattern of one type or another, whether a methodically planned, organized city or a messy and frenzied city. The pattern is the layout, the architecture, pedestrian transportation, services, culture, and the people.

Exploring these components by da Vinci is one more attempt and effort at pattern recognition that reflected his search for patterns in his surroundings and environment.

Whether da Vinci made mistakes, actually implemented thought-out principles, or continued with visions of the future city, he knew that those after him, in time, would learn from all of this. It is often thought that we make too little use of insights like da Vinci's that already exist. We must learn from great people of the past. We must learn from Leonardo da Vinci.

Today, he would be right in the middle of classic da Vinci mindset and imagining a world that was different from the one he lived in.

Da Vinci was once again, ahead of his time, this time with an urban planner hat on.

Obviously, many concepts regarding cities, traffic flow, and streets probably would have appeared strange to da Vinci in his time, but his forward thinking wrapped around his power of observation would bring all that forward. Leonardo would observe, while on foot, today, walking the streets, alleyways and open areas of the city he landed in, those things that five centuries ago would be different. He would observe streets, some wide, some narrow, with divided pathways for vehicles traveling in different, opposite directions: divided traffic. Back then he didn't use or even know the label of "vehicle," but would recognize terms like transporter, people mover, shipping vessels (land, not sea), and of course, horse and mule. He would observe, outside of the divided traffic ways, areas for those walking about: pedestrian walkways. He would be astounded at the volume of "traffic," the number of roads in all directions, and their organization. The thinking world truly revolved around how one would find their way. He would wonder how traffic stayed organized: Were there rules of the road; how did people learn them, know them, and apply them? Simple transporting and traffic flow would conjure up a whole new world of observation and thinking.

Da Vinci, currently observing, could relate back to the year 1502. In this year, using a compass, he produced a satellite-like image and view of the Italian town of Imola. This was the first map of this type in its time. Come on GPS!

Da Vinci sought to portray and represent the proportions and relationships between land and surroundings accurately, and some say he had to develop new technologies to do so: a compass to determine orientations, an instrument to capture the angles of streets, and a self-made odometer to measure distances from point to point. With careful measurements and new technology in hand, he drew every street, alleyway, parcel of land, building, church, and square of the city.

He provided a view of the city of Imola ichnographically, as if viewed from many viewpoints, true to geometric scale.

Da Vinci would recall this and apply it immediately to what he was seeing with streets, buildings, and land areas in today's world. If, for some reason, someone overlaid a satellite image of anything taken from outer space, he would be very interested, but not very surprised. His drawing of Imola was the predecessor to today's satellite images. Mapping a city of busy streets, buildings and surrounding areas was just another matter of course on this futuristic visit for da Vinci.

Sticking with his immersion into this New World and filling his mind with new perspectives, his eyes and thoughts would jump from the streets to the surrounding vertical and horizontal buildings.

"Just look at the buildings!" you can almost hear him exclaim. The size, the concentration of them, the shapes, the engineering, the functions, all would fuel his curiosity. That's the way his mind worked. Where do the people come from, that go in and out of these buildings? Don't they have crops to tend to, crafts to make, cities to govern, families to care for, art to be created? There were no animals in these buildings. The horseless wagons were powered vehicles: cars, trucks, and buses, as we know them today. Hard, rock flat, sturdy surfaces free of mud, clumps, imperfections and unevenness were abundant almost as if they continued on and on, endlessly.

His questions would flow, and in fact, overflow. Why are there porcelain receptacles in a room with another receptacle for flowing water? Was there really one for human waste discharge and the other for cleansing? He might ask related questions: Where did the water come from? Where did it go? Why is some hot and some cold? He would ask about the bar of wax-like material (soap) present instead of traditional Renaissance lye. He would also, as during his time, study the patterns of flow and the patterns of standing water. That was one of his earlier interests of nature and one that he continued to study.

And the glass! Da Vinci would learn more and see more windows than he ever thought imaginable. The one constant of viewing buildings of today and consistent with da Vinci's observations is the amount of glass in today's building. Flat, colorless panes, not the mosaics, crystal, ornamental plate ware of Renaissance days, but flat clear glass allowing the passage of light, and views inward and outward. Buildings with rooms would be lit not with flames but with ever-burning tubes. Doorways leading from one room to the next, all the things we take for granted, today. He would immerse his thinking into the architectural and design possibilities.

Da Vinci would be astonished and immediately start thinking of light passage, sunlight in particular. He would then further his thoughts by thinking about the temperature changes within a glass enclosed building and the wonderment of what happens upon darkness. He hadn't yet, but it wouldn't take long to connect darkness with electric lights.

Da Vinci would look at all the buildings, all the windows, and all the glass and be sharp enough to ask how inside temperature was controlled. Glare also was apparent and probably would be asked about. He would learn that man-made, mechanical temperature control (heat and air conditioning) would be the solution for the abundance of glass and building temperature.

Glass has always been a questionable material for use in large buildings in mass proportions because of that issue of controlling temperature, not to mention glare and reflection. Da Vinci's observations and curiosity would feed right into this notion. How would these buildings be cooled in the hot weather and conversely what about needed warmth in different seasonal times?

In looking at past da Vinci drawings and sketches, one could see familiarities in present day buildings: doorways, windows, staircases, ornamentation, roof structure and more architectural detail, probably for individual structures versus groups.

Leonardo would think immediately back to his many notebook drawings, sketches, doodles, and lists, and associate these familiarities.

Both the artist and the engineer were evident in his architectural drawings, notebook sketches, and more. Da Vinci's drawings of designs for buildings, bridges, streets, and structures of all types would lead to what he termed complete, "visionary" cities.

His ideas and drawings gave ideas on the "workings" of a building in addition to its outward physical appearance and sometimes beauty. After all, he was an artist as well as an engineer.

One vision Leonardo tried for, in Renaissance times, was an ideal city built on several levels with connecting vertical staircases. Leonardo suggested the placement of stairs outside of buildings, primarily to give more space to the interior spaces of buildings. He also wanted to make various levels accessed from houses.

Looking around, today, these building types would be present in abundance. Back in da Vinci's time, that vision was classified as unconventional. He was ahead of his time then, and his designs helped shape the styles that he would lay eyes on in his visit to today.

All this was at the outset of Leonardo's current, present day, city observation. For, at one time (da Vinci's time) he had envisioned an ideal city. Those many thoughts would come back to him and be compared and contrasted as he walked the earth, in present-day's time.

As his visit continued, he would watch daily life unfold before his eyes; the particulars of a general world evolving. He would be highly desirous of understanding as much of the how and why as he could. While he realized the totality of his desire, much would have to be researched after the initial observational part of his visit.

PART III

PEOPLE/FAMILIES

The sheer volume of people roaming around in present day is enormous. One quick thing Leonardo would notice is that there appears to be more "older" people than he was used to seeing. He wouldn't be sure why until he made one of his connected thoughts. He would observe that the older people were of the age of 60, 70, and 80 years plus. There were few of this age in Renaissance times, even though he, himself, lived to 67. The average life expectancy back then was 40, not old or old-appearing as he saw now in his casual observations.

He also saw more women than he was used to. Women of his time stayed home. They were, for the most part, homemakers and mothers. Men worked on farms, in the fields or at the local merchant shops. Of course, this varied by the class of people.

Leonardo would start to see, almost immediately, the material possessions that people had in terms of clothes, accessories, tools, and gadgets. A typical Renaissance family had far fewer possessions. Typically, they owned one or two changes of clothes, a single pair of shoes, food preparation utensils (not forks and spoons), pots for cooking and boiling, a bed, dining table, and places to sit at that table. Children had some games and a toy. Men had some tools and most possessions, certainly any extra possessions, were stored in a small footlocker/chest.

Family connections were important. With his many siblings, a young stepmother and a pre-occupied, professional father, Leonardo's immediate family connections were less than desirable. Leonardo was more looked after by his uncle, his father's brother, than his father. At least he had this as a family connection growing up.

Thinking about family, thinking about the over-abundance of people, he would revisit his familiar Renaissance times. Things sure were different today, but in many good ways. Just looking at a child's life in Renaissance times gave him one perspective to help him think about current times.

During Renaissance times, 20% of children died at birth. Homeschooling was popular for Renaissance families before children reached school age. That was typically around seven years of age. They woke up at first light, said prayers, washed up, dressed, ate a light breakfast, and went to a school class at 6:00 am. Typically, lunch was before the noon hour and dinner would be right at the five o'clock hour. Children's bedtime was before sunset every night as they would wake very early in the morning.

Was this how children spent their day in today's time? What was the mother's role? Was this same structure in place? After a brief bit of thought, he had the same questions as they related to an adult's life.

Da Vinci would be right at home in today's world in terms of friends and socializing. There would be lots of people around in today's times who shared the same thirst for knowledge, the same drive for innovation, and the same hope for improved lives as da Vinci did. He would love round table chats, coffee house get-togethers, not to mention all the socializing now done online in terms of social media.

Now with these perspectives as his base for people watching in his new world, Leonardo would pay attention to things like what people ate, where they went, which buildings they went in and out of and why, how they spent time with their families, where they worked to earn money, how they dressed, how they spent their off time, how they socialized, and how they interacted with others. He would look for that sense of harmony among families, for back in his time, that harmony wasn't always easy given the many adversities of Renaissance times.

In Renaissance times, there was a sense that families had to fight for survival. Viewing today's situations and families, Leonardo would see this characteristic as families and even individuals live pay check to pay check. That was part of the reason he would ask questions: Where people worked, where they went, why they did what they did on a routine, daily basis. In modern times, family and people would present a unique microcosm of daily events worth watching and worth its own separate observations and study.

SCHOOLS/ EDUCATION

The Renaissance period is known as a time where everyone was learning: men, women, and children. They didn't attend schools like those in today's times. Public schools had not been invented or developed yet. Much of the education came from the home front, associating with others, and apprenticeships with senior craftsmen and trades people. Many people were educated, but never attended school.

Da Vinci didn't go to school as we know it today. He never learned English. He received no formal education beyond basic reading, writing, and math on his way to becoming an art studio apprentice. He did read a lot, especially any Greek and Roman classics that he could collect.

Starting in late Renaissance times, Latin was replaced, initially by different dialects of the Italian language.

Italian is considered to be a direct branch of the Latin language spoken by the Romans and pushed on the citizens under their rule. Italian, though, is unique in that it is the language with the closest resemblance to Latin, even with the many dialects.

During the 14th century, the Tuscan dialect began to dominate. The Tuscany region was central in Italy because of its inclusion of Florence and all of its people and commerce.

Da Vinci spoke Italian, mostly as it is spoken now. He always talked about wanting to learn Latin as it would put him closer to the scholars of that time. Upon close inspection of some of the notes in his notebooks where he attempted to use Latin, he apparently failed or was less than fluent in the language. While he kept trying to learn Latin and even Classical Greek, he stuck with his Tuscany dialect of the Italian language. In everyday life he spoke, wrote, and understood modern day Italian just as anyone else would.

Visiting in today's world, even allowing for the translation quirks from English to Italian, da Vinci would hear and wonder about many expressions that would seem strange to him:

- Catch you later
- Hit me up
- I'll ring you later (although many cell phone users don't get this one anymore)
- What's up?

- Oh, my God
- You bet
- No worries
- My bad
- Grab some grub

Andrea del Verrocchio, artist, art teacher, and art mentor was impressed with the very early accomplishments of Leonardo. He urged Leonardo's father to enroll him to be further educated in del Verrocchio's workshop. This appealed to Leonardo and he set off to learn and practice anything and everything art-related in which design had a part. His father also recognized how talented the boy was at a young age; he had him study design, and the results of such an education can clearly be seen in his legacy. It wasn't a formal, university education but an education of doing, observing, and participating. People of the time learned trades from a master who had expertise in their field of study and who was skilled at a specific trade. Da Vinci learned from del Verrocchio. He studied in Verrocchio's workshop for over 10 years in the mid 15th century.

Leonardo would look around in new times for apprentice shops and mentors. Mentors exist, but in the form of school teachers, university professors, and business and trades people. Sometimes you can easily tell people are mentors and sometimes that is not obvious, except to the student.

As Leonardo stepped foot in current times, he would see a whole different educational system. He would see schools for younger children, colleges, and universities for those that were older and more progressed. These might appeal to him, but da Vinci would probably prefer studying things on his own, especially once he discovered how accessible information is through the Internet and vast libraries. He would continue his focus on observation, experimentation, and notebook entries. He would pursue technological learning, scientific subjects as well as the creative disciplines of graphics, video, photography, and art, which were his primary interests outside of inventing.

During Renaissance times da Vinci witnessed education taking on a different form. Humanism started influencing education.

Humanists during the Renaissance believed that education could reform and boost citizens personally and even help them with their duties to their communities. The subjects studied at this time were largely concerned with humanities such as poetry, moral philosophy, rhetoric, and grammar as well as the writings and studies of ancient authors. That was a contribution to the generally held concept that the Renaissance was a rebirth in understanding the educational practices of great civilizations prior.

Citizens' education in a K-12 system today elaborates on the fundamentals that da Vinci believed in and learned in that course called life and experience. He also learned it in his association with others during his apprenticeship. Da Vinci, upon further investigation and study, would see apprenticeships during modern times. In new times, he would see apprenticeships take the form of internships, entry level jobs, and structure within manual labor, craft, and trade jobs. This would satisfy da Vinci and his eagerness for education to attain reformations of citizens personally in their duties to their communities and fellow men, even in new times.

WORK/JOBS/
COMMISSIONS

Visiting the 21st century, Da Vinci would see buildings, he'd see nature, he'd see transportation and all things related to active city life. What would also be most abundant is the hustle and bustle as the throngs of people moved all about. Hustle and bustle is defined as a large amount of activity and work, usually in a noisy surrounding. That's exactly what da Vinci would see. It would be noticed and carefully observed.

Seeing the people, many thoughts would come to mind: Why so many, where are they going, do they work, are they friends and friendly? Could they be related? Could I meet them and carry on a conversation with them (language aside)?

Modern day people, during the day's observation, were mostly coming and going to work. Work in these days is different from work in Renaissance times.

In Renaissance days, the poorer, lower classes of people would be working on the streets, cleaning and selling things to make money, and working the fields of the wealthy.

When da Vinci thought about "work," he either thought of poor peasants working in the streets and fields, others in a higher stature job, or commissions for artists.

Higher stature jobs consisted typically of work from patrons that belonged as part of a guild, a specialized group with a focus on a niche of work. They were also known as an association of craftsmen or merchants, for the pursuit of a common goal, usually a vocational or trade goal.

Examples of guild work and other work of similar stature were:

- Wool Guild: Shearing of sheep and wool production

- Silk Guild: Trading and producing silk

- Guild of Furriers and Skinners: Producing animal furs and skins, mostly for clothing

- Guild of Bankers, Moneychangers: Managers of their own banks (bankers); exchanging different currencies, loaning money

- Guild of Druggists: Pharmacist or retailer of medicinal drugs available during those times

- Guild of Notaries: Legal experts and those authorized to perform certain legal functions and formalities

- Guild of Merchants: Trading of goods

All were ways that Renaissance people of the middle class made money.

The middle class rose in the early Renaissance partially as a result of the increase in bank, city, and urban expansion. Because of their accumulated wealth, this class of people was able to afford education, which resulted in better jobs than those in the lower classes. These jobs were reflected in the many guilds described above.

Leonardo earned his money in many ways: as a Renaissance entrepreneur, as an engineer, architect, and as advisor to the Italian royalty and stately lords. These included the Medici in Florence and the Sforza in Milan.

Leonardo got paid for advising on water management issues like well construction and canalization in Florence. These money-making projects for Leonardo sustained his lifestyle, hobbies, crafts, and artwork.

He worked on commission. Patrons (usually wealthy families) would commission art pieces from him and pay his living expenses while he worked on his art. He sometimes would also receive salary, pensions, and other remuneration from those who commissioned him. His work was in demand and patrons paid him well in order to acquire his services. Leonardo was also commissioned by certain religious orders and groups to complete paintings for them.

Da Vinci was able to survive as an artist with his commissions even though he left much work unfinished. Because the few works he was able to finish were so spectacular, he was glorified. It was fashionable in Renaissance times to be patronized as a famous artist and craftsman. The incompletion of his works was mostly overlooked. Today, da Vinci would learn and maybe learn hard that procrastination in any work is not tolerated or viewed upon favorably as it was in his day.

Consistent with his ongoing observations of modern times and when thinking about work and commissions, da Vinci would certainly ask if there were any painters or artists in the throngs of people he observed. If so, did they receive commissions? Who would commission them to paint in today's times? Who were their patrons? Were commissions enough to live on? Da Vinci was never at a loss for questions to ask, especially when introduced to new things.

Leonardo da Vinci received a commission to paint his "Adoration of the Magi" from the Augustinian monks of San Donato in Scopeto just outside of Florence, who planned to use it as an altarpiece. This artwork is historically significant by virtue of the artistic conventions and innovations da Vinci made that were unique during his time. This fueled his reputation then and ongoing.

Another commission was for a painting that was to be completed in the Altar of St. Bernard Chapel in the Palazzo della Signoria in Florence. The painting was never begun and other, earlier commissions were never completed. He was known for unfinished work, but still received commissions.

Leonardo's commissions seemed to keep coming. Right after the turn of the century, in 1503, Leonardo received a commission to paint a mural for the council hall in Florence's Palazzo Vecchio. This was deemed a prized commission for a well-known historical event. For three years, he worked on this, known as the Battle of Anghiari. At the same time, Michelangelo worked on a complementary (and competing) painting, depicting a scene from the Battle of Cascina. Both paintings remained unfinished.

Like other Renaissance painters, da Vinci focused on religious or semi-religious images and symbols used in his works of art and the study or interpretation of these within his themes, but he also did portraiture, which was an important part of his income during his life.

One portrait commission was given to Leonardo by Francesco del Giocondo, a successful Florentine merchant. Giocondo wanted something in return for his advocacy of Leonardo's talents. He wanted a small portrait painted of his young wife, Lisa del Giocondo. Little did either know that the portrait would go on to become the most famous painting of all time, The Mona Lisa. Da Vinci might observe in new times many people, many expressions, many personalities that he would love to use in portraiture painting. Upon further investigation into this, he would see a dominance in this area by commercial personal photography in place of painted portraits.

Renaissance artists worked with many patrons to fund them and commission their work. This included working with political leaders, the wealthy and privileged few, nobility and royalty, government officials, and the Catholic Church.

Most of this backing in the arts came from rich, upper class families, who either championed artists through their own family collections or through the Church.

Some of the other prominent patrons of the arts were the actual city-states such as Florence. Florence sanctioned the creation of multiple statues of David during Renaissance years. These can now be seen all around the city of Florence and nearby regions. Where were the statues in modern times in his new city? They aren't as abundant and he would be curious as to why.

Leonardo was an artist first, in order to support himself. He did frequent commissions, but he made most of his money from civil and military engineering. He was constantly in demand because "he worked hard to make sure he was in demand," working in many areas, with many focuses, on many projects for many people. That was his idea of work then and he would be interested in how it was approached today. It didn't quite appear that people always worked that hard. Mental work was different than work requiring dexterity.

The Renaissance period showed us that there was more than one type of patron or sponsor. While patronage today is virtually synonymous with "getting money from those that have it, in return for what you have," much of the patronage of the Renaissance for painting was paid for by the church, with many of Florence's most significant public treasures paid for by its various guilds. It was a period every bit as obsessed with money as our period of time today. Their times were also a period when the most powerful institutions in society saw the creation of art as central to their missions, causes, and identity.

Money was a means to an end. Simply sponsoring art was the ticket by which money transformed into meaning for people's lives.

There were other da Vinci commissions, some notable and now famous. Da Vinci would wonder not only "where all these people worked and how they made money to seek their ends," but also he would think, "where did artist's commissions come from?" He wouldn't see a lot of artists so he had to wonder where the commissions were.

Since artistry was a vocation, especially during Renaissance times, surely it had to make a large part of today's world and be part of the make-up of all the people hustling and bustling. This would beg many, many questions related to the people, their art-related jobs, vocations, and all that they did to earn money.

Here are his observations of the hustle and bustle, related to working people and potential art commissions:

- Do the artists see the science
  in all that they do?

- Do the scientists see the art
  in all that they do?

- Are there scientists walking around that
  could translate their thoughts into art?

- How come no one carries around
  a sketchbook on their belt?

- Why aren't people sitting and
  staring and sketching?

- Where is all the observation of nature,
  people, and mechanical items?

- With all these cubes, curves, natural
  life, and people, the opportunity for
  sketching and eventually high quality art
  seems endless. Why isn't there more?

- There are so many variations of
  expressions, dress, activity and more that
  all goes into artistry of any time, then
  and now. How can this be captured?

- What is this concept of a photograph?
  Is it a painting? How come there are
  so many? How are they produced/
  reproduced if painted or not? How
  do people review them again?

- Where are all the work studios for artists?

- Where do all the colors come from?
  Are the paints, pigments, and dyes
  made from chalk, oil, water, lye, or
  some other base material? Do the artists
  concoct and mix them for their use?

- Are all these pictures moneymakers
  for someone or have they been
  sponsored by some citizen patron?

- Does art apprenticeship work
  like what I went through?

- Are there apprenticeships for every job?

There is just so much to see, to absorb, to compare and contrast and to learn from, to make things better. Lots of people, lots of work, lots of visuals.

RENAISSANCE MAN VS. SPECIALIST

By now you are learning that Leonardo fits the exact definition of a Renaissance man: someone of many talents with many areas of knowledge. He lived his life believing that man had the capacity for the ultimate in personal development that could expand with no limits. That is right in line with Renaissance thinking where those in that time lived the philosophy of always trying to reach their fullest potential in life. In order to do that, one must participate in the creative part of art, keeping of fit mind and body, and pursuing what is right for them emotionally. This was a way that considered complete wholeness in life in many different forms.

Leonardo was known for his legendary art skills producing many masterpieces. We know him, still to this day, 500+ years after his death, as the artist behind The Mona Lisa, The Last Supper, and the Vitruvian Man: truly timeless masterpieces. If only his inventions were actually produced and left in a form for all to see, experience, and learn from versus just sketches of them. He would see, from his visit to current times, that technology would have advanced more quickly to the point where it is today.

Disregarding the fact that his inventions never did make it to real form, Leonardo's brilliance of mind, relentless curiosity, and passion for knowledge still stood out for this Renaissance genius.

It was his choice to live boldly and in the way he did, consistent with his identity (now) of being a true Renaissance Man. He would subscribe to the un-ending continuous development and relentless curiosity, knowing there was still so much to learn in the world around him.

Renaissance men are unique. Not everyone had a diverse set of interests nor did they pursue them even if they did. Those that did could connect and combine their diverse knowledge and produce incomparable solutions making all with Renaissance characteristics, invaluable.

The other inherent component that was invaluable was that Renaissance men are unconstrained by the viewpoints that specialists have that are narrow, focused, and many times, tunnel vision-like. Renaissance men view things much more broadly, looking at many angles for many opportunities, regardless of the objective.

In viewing today's world, Leonardo would see focuses different from his focus. Today, there would be people with a personal and work focus, while developing specialized skills related to that concentration. Mostly this is in the area of jobs and employment. As Leonardo showed, there's tremendous value in expanding one's mind by studying subjects completely unrelated to their primary field of study or interest, connecting with what is already known and developing a broad base of skills and talents.

Da Vinci would see teachings in today's schools to develop students to be very good at a very specific trade or skill as a very narrow focus, a specialization approach. That was not the case in da Vinci's day. What ultimately propelled da Vinci to be the best artist he could be was knowledge of other subjects, related and unrelated to art and painting. That in turn turned him into a great scientist, inventor, and much more as you have seen.

Many people now would say to da Vinci that he is distracted by having too many areas of focus and interests, but he would counter that by saying his prolific success then and now is because he is multi-disciplined. (The term Renaissance man was unknown to da Vinci but the definition described here was not.)

Da Vinci firmly believed that learning directly was not always the key. What was key was learning things that helped expand how one thinks and one's perspective on everything to know about life and the world we live in, then and now.

Today, we see often the revival of the Renaissance man (or woman), reinvented as more of an entrepreneurial innovator. In today's time, he would also quickly learn of the term entrepreneur.

Religion

It is important to note here that Leonardo had an unconventional state of mind when it came to religion. So great was his interest and curiosity about how things worked that he would believe only what had been proved and experienced first-hand before his eyes.

Leonardo's notebook entries indicate that he based his beliefs on reason. Reason is considered one's ability to perceive reality as honestly and completely as one can. From this logic, conclusions can be made based on those perceptions. Leonardo valued reason much more than faith.

Leonardo had solid knowledge of religious allegory and contemporary church teachings, which he combined with a humanistic approach to his art's subjects. Just look at The Last Supper.

How could the artist responsible for some of the best-known images of Christian art not have been a

Christian himself? Regardless of his beliefs, his goal was to transform the traditional view of The Last Supper into a more human-centered, emotion-filled drama.

Da Vinci stepped aside from religious tendencies and commandments to focus on everyday life: the challenges, problems, needs, and opportunities. That could be said about most of da Vinci's life and experiences. That was the early humanistic approach of Renaissance times.

Looking around today, da Vinci had already seen the plethora of buildings: commercial, homes, "institutional," retail, and more. Then he would start to recognize the many churches amongst the landscape. He would immediately shift into religious-thinking mode and try to assimilate what he knew from Renaissance times to what he now saw in modern times. In order to do that he would have to revisit, even if within his own mind, his stance on religion, participation, support, and benefit from all things religious in his time.

Many of the great painters of da Vinci's time focused on religious themes and settings and were often commissioned by the church and church-related patrons, including the Pope himself. Churches were huge patrons of the arts and architecture, and purchased tremendous amounts of art to create admiration, reverence, and respect. The Catholic Church, in particular, often commissioned large scale works, frescos of the life of Christ, religious events and scenes, the Virgin Mary, or the life of a Catholic saint. Churches also commissioned altarpieces and small devotional pictures.

Da Vinci would wonder why all the non-religious paintings hung in the many types of buildings and dwellings he saw today. There were some with religious tones, but nothing like he was used to seeing or painting back in his days.

Religion was part of everyday life in his time, deeply connecting painters, architects (like da Vinci), and those they worked for. Many of the religious paintings of the time are among the greatest works of art, not just of Renaissance times, but all time. The tie to religion was very obvious and evident. The same goes for much of the architecture of the time. Leonardo also designed churches in his architectural pursuits.

While there is an abundance of churches in today's times, they do not all look alike and many take on new and abstract forms.

Was Leonardo da Vinci religious? Art historian Luke Syson has stated that, "Leonardo had solid knowledge of *religious* symbolism and contemporary Catholic teachings, which he combined with a humanistic approach to his arts subjects." Leonardo's greatest works were the fruit of his engagement with religious subjects, entrusted to him by some of the Renaissance's most rigorous and religious patrons.

Leonardo said very little about religion anywhere in his notebooks. Even with all the church architecture and images of religious figures, sketches and notes were minimal.

Does this mean he gave religion little thought? Is it because he could not explain or express his religious thought? He basically treated explanations and expressions, and the respective sketches and notes related to his emotions the same. Did da Vinci so often fail to record his own emotions or declare his own feelings, especially about religion, for fear others would consider him heretical? He would be in more of a comfort zone in today's time when the subject of religion came up or was encountered.

Giorgio Vasari, famed da Vinci biographer from the 16th century, wrote:

> *"Leonardo's cast of mind was so heretical that he did not adhere to any religion, thinking perhaps that it was better to be a philosopher than a Christian."*

That being said, he was probably more religious than all of history has given him credit for, including Vasari. Take his personal library, for instance. The religious literature stacked on his home library bookshelves is rarely mentioned. He had a large assortment of religious books in his personal library and even though limited, he is known to have made regular references in his own notebooks to religious ideas. A passionate and devoted reader, Leonardo owned several Bibles in Italian along with writings by St. Augustine, St. Albert the Great, and a volume of Psalms amid his collection of books.

Leonardo was probably a Christian given the strong influence in his times. He was not, however, beholden to the same Roman Catholic world view as all others (which probably accounts for Vasari's statement). He believed in experimentation, observation, and scientifically testing hypotheses. In doing so, many times, he would come up with some results that the Church was not in favor of or that opposed some of their teachings. Leonardo valued reason much more than faith. The Church did not. Regardless, his paintings were of religious figures and had religious overtones which the Church did like and which kept da Vinci in their favor.

During da Vinci's lifetime—from 1452 to 1519—there were 10 different popes. Da Vinci's relationship to the Catholic Church involved a thoughtful balance between his scientific zeal and the intensity with which he explored the ideas surrounding religious beliefs and, of course, any patronage he could garner.

During the part of Renaissance time that da Vinci lived, he was free from extreme religious persecution in Europe. Most other people of his time were devoutly religious, including writers, artists, and philosophers with their references to God. The fact that he made little reference to the divine in all his writing and notes suggests he saw less use for a traditional allegiance or worship of God. Along the way in his new journey, he would meet many people of the same ilk. Sure, there are many who are very devout but being less than devout is more accepted in modern times.

During the Renaissance period in Italy, the growth of an idea called Humanism began. This was a time period when man focused on his own enlightenment and less on religious implications while questioning the role and involvement of the Catholic Church.

Even though much Renaissance art was inspired by religious themes, there was a leaning towards the human representation of religion; a drifting towards Humanism.

Leonardo was interested in a Renaissance worldview which centered around the human person. This interest resulted in his works depicting a natural view of man and the human body and one that explored the personalities of the individuals he drew, sketched, and painted. These are evident in his masterpieces, sketches, notes, and even his unfinished work.

Da Vinci's commitment to scientific investigation and experimentation led him to cast doubt on certain stories found in the Bible. His religious paintings were driven by the system of patronage in Italy that paid him the commissions for painting such pictures. Whether da Vinci observed, practiced, or believed the fundamental principles of Catholicism is a debate that continues to this day.

Leonardo put far more faith in experience-based

knowledge than that of religious doctrine. This quote from him says it all:

> *"It seems to me that all studies are vain and full of errors unless they are based on experience and can be tested by experiment, in other words, they can be demonstrated to our senses. For if we are doubtful of what our senses perceive then how much more doubtful should we be of things that our senses cannot perceive, like the nature of God and the soul and other such things over which there are endless disputes and controversies."*

This indicates more conclusively that Leonardo, while likely a believer in God and an aficionado of religion, distanced himself from religion and defaulted to realistic, experience-based approaches to his faith.

There was, however, religion from beginning to end for Leonardo. He was baptized as an infant in front of family and friends. As he approached the end of his life, he lay sick for many months. When he found himself on death's bed, he made every effort to learn more about the doctrine of Catholic ritual. Da Vinci asked for a priest to hear his last confession and administer the Last Rites. He died in early May of 1519 and was given a Catholic funeral, received the sacraments of the Church, and was buried in consecrated ground.

Religion or Science

In 1517, two years before da Vinci would die, Martin Luther, a German monk, led the Protestant Reformation—a revolutionary movement that caused a split in the Catholic Church. Many saw the Catholic Church as less than fit for the religious obligations and callings and felt it needed reform. The Reformation did not impact Italy as much as other European countries or regions. By 1600, Protestantism was effectively extinct in Italy. This was all at the tail end of da Vinci's life and passed by with his eye on other priorities.

The Protestant Reformation caused many, many Europeans to leave the Catholic Church. I mention this because walking and observing in today's time in any common city, many religions, among them Catholicism and Protestantism, would be in view.

What da Vinci would soon come to realize is that three quarters of the population were Christians, with 50% claiming to be Protestants and close to 25% being Catholic. But Christianity would be very different from the churches, altars and cathedrals that he was used to.

Today, each religion and there are many, builds their own temples and churches. Sometimes walking the city these are quite evident; sometimes they aren't.

Da Vinci would notice the shift to Protestantism but, not knowing about Martin Luther and the Reformation, he would therefore be very quizzical and question the role of the Catholic Church here. Even though he wasn't overly religious, he would want to understand the differences, reasons why the shift occurred, what that did to art patronage, what was to be painted, who would do the commissioning, and where the paintings would hang for all to see. He would see examples and paintings on display, some like he was used to, but many that he wasn't used to. He certainly would not see the dominance of religious art, in the form he knew, as he did in Renaissance times.

As he tried to understand these differences and the effect on art he would also see and want to understand other related things:

- Church attendance
- Places of worship
- Spirituality not religion
- Many religions although mostly Christian
- A predominance of Protestants
- Interfaith across the country
- Megachurches
- Online worship
- Women in clergy positions
- A Non-Italian pope
- Catholicism's effect worldwide
- Churches fitting in to the modern urban landscape

Churches are different. The effect is similar, but with a different slant. Da Vinci would have to learn this, understand this, and understand the effect on all the things that the Church that he knew of in his time had. He would have to adapt, ignore or embrace at a whole different, elevated level. Given the variety of churches and religions, chances are he would be in an adaptive mode. The influences in modern times would not necessarily be less, but they would be spread out, less concentrated, and divided among the many. Da Vinci would be fine in this area at this time.

MEDICAL

During Renaissance times, infections and infectious diseases were not known about other than those that people contracted. Cures, medicines, and diagnosis were mostly absent. Da Vinci's observation of a current time's doctor swabbing the throat of a sick patient and analyzing the culture would be a feat of amazement and astonishment. It still is today, as most do not know the science or inner biological workings of such. His question would be: How could a doctor or medical professional tell from a simple test what was wrong and have a potential cure? Nice to be living in these times today. In the back of his mind, he probably thought about how many lives would have been saved if today's doctors and medical methods and treatments were available for those contracting the plague.

With Leonardo's attitude towards health and well-being, he would surely want to know if everyone in sight was healthy. Did anybody have diseases? What would ill health's effect be on people? Would they be in danger of things like the Great Plague that ravished Renaissance times in the 13th and 14th century? What wisdom could he offer to further the health and well-being and hygiene of those walking the current planet?

Before the Coronavirus pandemic of 2020, the greatest plague in history was The Black Death of 1347-1351. Although it arose in China, it spread to Europe with destructive consequences. Renaissance Italians were not excluded. The population of Florence alone was reduced by over 50%. Outbreaks continued in Europe for a very long time afterwards.

Did the Black Death period actually give birth to the Renaissance? Would da Vinci look at today's outbreaks and think the same? Little did da Vinci realize that the world is now in a position to limit and contain damage by plague-like diseases. Those scientists and medical professionals that came after da Vinci made life safer.

Leonardo realized, during his time, that the crowded streets, cramped living conditions, and overstuffed housing could contribute to the spread of disease. He stated that when he designed the ideal city, his designs for cities took into consideration sanitation, natural beauty, and the operation and flow, with an emphasis on good health. This contributed to his preaching of learning to preserve health and to take responsibility for wellness through nutrition, exercise, and other factors of a healthy lifestyle. Important then and most important now.

Da Vinci's health prescription didn't look any different than what we see today: Drink plenty of water, exercise and move the body, rest, relax and enjoy the pleasures of life, and take full advantage of our natural surroundings. Da Vinci encouraged positive thinking. He knew that it contributed to health or at least quicker recoveries to ill health. With all that da Vinci did mentally, his mental health was probably at a record high for being well maintained.

Da Vinci would look for these things along his path in today's time. Is the food being served nutritious and balanced? Is there opportunity to take care of the physical needs of good health? Are we all working towards a common goal of taking care of others? Do others share information, cures, and thoughts on keeping healthy and promoting health?

Leonardo talked about sickness as "the discord of the elements of the human body," and healing as "the restoration of discordant elements."

He would take one look at sickness and suggest that now is the time for all to focus on getting discordant elements back in order. He would suggest solutions, even tactics such as working together to spur more creativity and innovation to fight current disease and ill being.

It's amazing how times have changed since the Renaissance period and how some things have not.

Da Vinci would be quick to realize this and offer what is proven and question what is not. That's his human nature; that's his curious mindset at work and that's life in the New World for da Vinci.

Da Vinci was also interested in health and well-being and the human specimen from an artistic point of view.

Da Vinci studied human anatomy and the human body's motion and mechanics in depth. He is well known for his anatomical sketches and studies of the human body. At that point in time, da Vinci's primary learning mechanism was dissecting human cadavers and then drawing what he saw. It is believed that da Vinci had grave robbers and eventually a hospital director procure cadavers to study. Where were cadavers supplied from today? How did medical professionals learn the inner workings of human anatomy? These would be current curiosities, for sure.

Before the advent of modern imaging, dissections revealed the complicated inner workings of the human body when there was no other way. Da Vinci yearned to witness these mechanics for himself. Though he lacked any formal medical training, he is believed to have dissected more than 30 bodies in his lifetime, leaving behind, in his notebooks, many accurate anatomical drawings.

As an artist, scientist, and engineer, da Vinci wanted to know not only how the human body was constructed, how it worked, and the anatomy behind it, but also where the emotions came from and how expressions worked.

He did this to aid his painting of people, their motion, and expressions. This was always on his mind and would be today as he saw the many people walking around and the many different presentations of people.

As he dove behind the scenes of today and learned more about medical technology, medical science, diagnostics, and treatment he would think back to his days of learning about human anatomy and the human mechanism of us all.

His trip around modern times would turn up things to help with understanding the human body, with understanding disease and in learning about wellness as opposed to just sickness. Da Vinci would see that stealing of corpses from cemeteries was not only not allowed, but not happening. What he would see would be things like MRI machines, X-ray technology in use, doctor's examinations, blood tests and more, related to diagnostics. These were late 19th and 20th century inventions, now in full use. Medical science advancement would boggle his mind and immediately make him wonder about disease control (like the Black Plague in pre-Renaissance times) and everyday health. With da Vinci being a big believer in wellness of the human body, mind, and spirit, he would wonder how such a thing was measured. Back in his times, measurement and assessment would be crude, especially compared to today's advancements. Here's what he would see: No more cadaver dissection. No more stealing bodies from morgues and cemeteries. He would see a separate health industry, all focused on the citizens that he always spoke of trying to help. Much of this help is now in their own hands. Physical fitness and nutrition fall into that category.

Leonardo would be pleased that upon his review of the medical world, that his anatomical studies still remain scientifically significant. Da Vinci would see that his drawings and studies hardly deviated from the way things are viewed today.

For instance, he correctly described the heart as the center of the blood system and was the first to describe it as a muscle with four chambers. He discovered how small vortices of blood help shut the aortic valve. There were many more contributions that could take over the focus of his visit, but so could all the topics he was curious in.

"He started with an interest of understanding the body to improve his art," explains *Decoding da Vinci* producer Doug Hamilton. "But he clearly went further. He clearly became fascinated by understanding the human body."

SPORTS AND FITNESS

"Da Vinci knew his body was a strong house for his creativity and took care of it by practicing the cultivation of grace, ambidexterity, fitness, and poise."

-Michael Gelb, *How to Think Like Leonardo da Vinci*

Among the citizens of Florence, da Vinci was renowned for his athleticism along with other physical qualities. His skill with horses was of a very high level and he was considered strong in his day. His strength and obsession with the human body, many have argued, were a basis for his passion for anatomy and the study and sketching of all things human body related.

He would observe, in new times, bodies of all shapes, sizes, and physical condition. He would even observe places where people were lifting heavy objects, evidently working on their strength and conditioning. It would be gratifying to see others cultivating their own grace, ambidexterity, and poise for better fitness. Very da Vinci like.

Back in Renaissance times, there were no organized sports and clubs as da Vinci would observe today.

During da Vinci's time, people spent much of their time doing physically demanding activities such as farming and other household chores. It was only natural, then, for people to relax with games and other things that gave them a break from the physically demanding activities. This suggested board games but not many contact sports as we know them today.

Athletic prowess, regular exercise, and physical maintenance took the form of swimming and walking. He would be pleased to see this still happening in modern times.

Da Vinci spoke much about it and believed that everyone should accept personal responsibility for their health and well-being. This was part of the contribution to his vegetarian beliefs. This also was part of some of his painting and sculpting techniques where both sides of his body were in play whether he was sketching, painting, or carving. It was no surprise that he would preach to many, "Learn to preserve your health!" He would be popular today with that mantra.

Today, da Vinci would observe more awareness of fitness and physical upkeep. In any typical city, he would see people running for fitness, walking for social communion, exercising with and without equipment, alone and in groups. He would see organized sports, teams, clubs, games, and activities. He wouldn't call this "sports," even though today the whole concept of team sports would be in play. Sports in his day were not common. If this genius and healthy, fit mind would have lived in the present time, sports would certainly have had his interest. He would want to know the why, the techniques, achievements, benefits, who participated and more about sporting activity; sports would be another thing to see that was new, to think about that was absent during his time, and to further thinking and perspectives with creativity and innovation beyond his curious spirit.

Da Vinci already realized the different food choices in new times. He would hope and probably see some foods related to nourishment and creating and maintaining a healthy, fit body.

FOOD

One observation within the bustling city life would be the smells, the tastes, the consumption, the preparation of all things food and nourishment related, for da Vinci knew that his ability to create relied on a healthy, fit body. He saw bigger and more modern office buildings. He saw new homes. He viewed retail shops. He now saw before him a third variety of buildings in the form of food establishments.

Da Vinci, as best he could understand in these new times, would observe that the food, given local tastes, was of high quality. Food items in Renaissance Italy were known for their freshness and quality, too. As best as he could comprehend, food items, in current times, were expensive. Much currency (or that infamous plastic card) was being traded in exchange for meal portions and packages.

The kind, quality, and quantity of food during the Renaissance depended on location and wealth. The average person of peasant stature would eat helpings of soup consisting of food scraps, vegetables, or eggs, and what they referred to as mush (similar to oatmeal). Some bread was available but not at every meal.

The wealthy would be used to large quantities and feast-like meals. Spices and sweetness prevailed amongst this class. So did the quantities and higher quality of meat.

In current times, representations and character of a city are food related. This not only involves the food itself but where it is served and how it is served. That's not much different from point to point in Renaissance days, but currently, there are many different choices and offerings. Call it culture through dining or culture through eating; much more of a food culture is present today than it was 500 years ago.

He would see sit-down dining halls (restaurants), walk up or drive through food stations, places to pick up and take away food, meals, and packaged food. These locations seemed endless. These locations offered much to touch the senses. Da Vinci was all about touching senses.

Da Vinci would look around and also notice a plethora of "drinking establishments." Some of these even served food in addition to drinks. His questions would start: Why so many? What are the differences? How do you choose one over another? Did they serve the same items? Do you just go and drink? These kinds of questions would undoubtedly run through his head when observing this one small city component. Cheers to the New World and new times!

Da Vinci understood drinking, as alcohol consumption during his time would be moderate and sometimes heavy. Many people of Renaissance times, both Protestant and Catholic, believed that God created alcohol to be consumed moderately, for pleasure, health, and enjoyment. Drunkenness and public intoxication were considered a sin back in his time. He would surely wonder at the extent of the sinfulness today.

Water was not of high quality during his time. Back then, it was even cut with wine or ale to make it tastier and safer.

While eating choices in the Italian Renaissance were the beginning of much of our modern food culture, da Vinci would look around at the many eating establishments and ask the same questions he did when thinking about and observing the drinking establishments.

Renaissance fare was a function of what the wealthy devised in his times. Da Vinci witnessed the start of this with the Medici family and other aristocrats and would see it in action throughout the variety of meal preparation and consumption in current times. Simple things like utensils and plates, abundant and taken for granted today, were just being invented by these lavish families at their stylish feasts and banquets. The fork is a prime example. In new times, da Vinci would surely see his share of forks, among other utensils, in full and regular use at every meal at every meal place. These and other kitchen gadgets would be right up his alley with all of his inventiveness, his mechanical mind, his curious mind, and his desire to always try to improve a process.

When da Vinci planned his feasts and mixed with royalty and the wealthy, he liked, of course, to eat what they ate. This consisted of green salads, fruit, fresh vegetables, bread, grains, and pasta. Because of his vegetarian tendencies, he would eat eggs, cheese, butter, and fig preserves and avoid the many meat delicacies.

Food was not a strange concept to da Vinci. The excess of establishments in a retail and grocery world would, though, be a bit strange to him today. His notebooks of yesteryear contained comments, grocery lists, prices, kitchen efficiency and design ideas, and even meal planning ideas (feasts vs. household fare). Translating to today's times would seem feasible short of a few customs and types of food.

Looking around today, almost in any city, one would see many places called "Italian Restaurants," that offer "Italian" fare. Today, that means pizza, meatballs, pasta, Stromboli, lasagna, and the like. Da Vinci would see this and recognize only a vague association with Italian fare of the Renaissance. Today we have tangy tomato sauce. Da Vinci would have vegetables like mushrooms, as well as wine, lemons, and classic Italian cheeses used in Renaissance concoctions, gently resembling today's menu items. His choice of meat (mostly for others), even though he was a vegetarian, would be spiced, minced, and prepared to come close to today's modern meatballs, but not the same. Pasta, for sure but not tomato sauce, not in the form that is known today.

Da Vinci's preference, whether consuming or preparing, was that meals should be "well-cooked and simple." He even wrote about this in his notebooks. He didn't dine on what we know as a classic pizza Napolitano or a tray of lasagna, but he probably would have approved today's great crust, perfectly spiced tomato sauce, creamy mozzarella and fresh basil. We call it pizza and pizza places dominate cities—they are on almost every street block. He didn't know the term pizza but he was familiar with oven-baked flat rounds of bread brushed with olive oil and dusted with some spices and herbs. That dish was popular even before pizza as we know it, was first made in Naples.

Leonardo ate a lot of spinach, too. Any food labeled "Florentine" means with spinach, and that's where he lived. He would see dinners ala Florentine on today's menus and instantly recognize this heritage-based dish and be very pleased.

Da Vinci would look at current food supply and servings in restaurants and tie and connect it all to experiences, expressions through food and atmosphere. He would pay attention to how food and meals were being served. He would grow to understand that dining, and really, the social side of dining, could produce experiences that take the place of things; very 21st century-like thinking. Of course, he would want to revamp anything Italian-oriented to reflect his times, bringing forth the past, but respectful of the current tastes.

All in all, da Vinci would be very interested and very, very curious about food as he valued its importance in daily life and well-being. He would see the variety of foods available today and be pleased. He could easily spend the rest of time exploring food, its preparation, nourishment, and serving and probably never satisfy his curiosity about this one topic. That could be said about anything under observation in these new times for him.

Trade/Retail/Shops

One thing evident during da Vinci's visit would be the sheer number of buildings, both residential and commercial. Commercial buildings would be in the form of restaurants, offices, and retail shops. Most of these would appear to be strange, once past the quantity overwhelm. Office buildings in Renaissance times were more an assemblage of work areas or work spaces. Botticelli's painting of St. Augustine showed one of these work spaces. The painting is one of St. Augustine, in his cell with a workspace consisting of a small, three-walled alcove with a curtain. This suggested that "office" work in Renaissance times was done in secluded spaces to maximize focus. These early "workstations" comprised a desk, chair, and storage shelves, with a curtain barrier. Coincidentally, this painting of St. Augustine in his office space hangs in the Uffizi Gallery, which was originally the central administrative building of the Medici empire in the mid 1550s.

This administrative building would lend familiarity to da Vinci. It resembled many of the "corporate" office structures da Vinci would observe along his journey. The building also served as both a workplace and a visible statement to the people as one of prestige and power. While seminaries and church buildings had these spaces, such spaces were rare in medieval times, as most people worked from home.

Remember, to compare something new, you have to think and remember the familiar and the past that influences current thinking and observation.

Looking back to Renaissance times, trade and commerce had a large presence and influence. Trade was popular during the Renaissance and starting to become more widespread, especially in the Italian cities of Genoa, Rome, Milan, and Florence, where trade flourished. Trade brought the people of this time wealth, which led them to more education and more appreciation of and study of the arts, things that the Renaissance is known for. Trade was an integral part of the culture of the regions and cities. From this came new ideas, new customs, and new ways of life. As a result of trade, the economy in Italy flourished. There was a concentration on money and currency exchange as the surrounding cities and region became more independent. Craftsmen, tradesmen, and merchants became more predominant as they realized more income and family wealth. This effect on the Renaissance was one of the reasons it was such a good time period to live in. Da Vinci would definitely vouch for that as would his fellow artists and citizens of the time. Da Vinci would see current life and wonder if the times were just as good with all the new things he observed. With da Vinci being da Vinci and with his mindset, the answer to that would be a definite yes and he was about to explore that.

What's important to note here is that the people of Renaissance Florence, like most cities and regions of that time, started the formation of social classes. Those of note were the nobles, the merchants, the tradesmen, and the skilled workers.

The tradesmen of Florence were the craft workers, shopkeepers, and merchants. Most tradesmen and merchants belonged to guilds, organizations that established standards of quality, trading rules, rules for membership, and treatment of outside competition. Guilds are an association of craftsmen or merchants formed for mutual aid, benefit, and protection while furthering their professional interests and crafts. These guilds were the purveyors of retail trade. The predominant guilds were the bankers, silk/textile, and wool merchants.

During the Renaissance, the European economy grew dramatically, particularly in the area of this described trade. Population growth, improvements in banking and financing, expanding trade routes to other regions and even other countries, and new crafting methods and systems led to an increase in commercial trade activity.

FLORENCE

Changes during this time, were taking place all over Europe with Florence being right in the center of Renaissance progression and cultural shifts.

Trade guilds controlled trade in the city and outside of the city, into and from other regions. The members of these guilds held and made most of the money and were significant members of the city's government.

Most powerful among the guilds were the textile workers. Florence was the center of cloth making and cloth trading. Wool of excellent quality came from England. In Florence, the raw material was cleaned, spun, dyed, and woven. Florence was known for the production of cloth, wool, silk, and other textile goods.

Da Vinci would observe all the different styles of clothing, colors, designs, shapes, and sizes that people in new times were wearing and try hard to reconcile all of that with the textile good trading that he was familiar with in Renaissance Florence. The missing piece for him in his reconciliation, was the manufacturing and distribution facilities piece, that were not present in Renaissance times nor necessarily needed. More learning available here for the master.

Another source of income that Florence was known for was banking. Many families of Florence were part of the banking trade. The most famous bankers were the Medici. They controlled Florence money, business, and politics up to the beginning of the 18th century. Da Vinci would be sure about money flow in new times. He would see currency and coins but he would also see plastic cards being used, more so than currency. Was this somehow tied to the packet of money and valuable for each person (known to all in modern times as bank accounts)?

Where did Renaissance citizens buy and sell goods? What could da Vinci familiarize himself with in his times to make a current comparison?

There were merchant stalls in city markets and shops along the way in Renaissance times, especially in Florence. The Ponte Vecchio spanning the River Arno was an astonishing bridge in Florence, lined with shops on both sides; mostly butchers serving the patrons of Florence as a walk-by market. This was more retail he could familiarize himself with.

There is detail from the 1470 Ferrarese frescoes of Palazzo Schifanoia showing busy retail shops with customers. "Retail Shopping" became a new activity and form of consumer behavior then, but wasn't referred to with those descriptions and terms. Da Vinci would witness what exploded into a full blown economic driver in today's world with all the retail and shopping going on.

The main driver of this retail direction in Renaissance times was the expanding power of the noble class in comparison to the Church. This resulted in a growing wealth, interest, and confidence of the Italian merchant/tradesman class. This was part of the humanism movement during that time, i.e., educated people becoming more interested in human rather than spiritual concerns and church emphasis.

Call it a secular ethic, but as part of humanism, there was a belief that worldly accomplishment and development and the associated wealth was equal to wars defending religion and the Church and praying. Merchants honored trade and wealth, and the earthly and spiritual goods that wealth could produce. This included the means to provide the family unit more for their well-being as well as providing for learning and art.

Da Vinci would clearly see a belief before him, in new times, that human needs and their accompanying values are more important than religious beliefs. There are still, in this time, religious beliefs, but humanism is on full display.

TRANSPORT/ CARS/VEHICLES

Not only would the number, size, shape, and functionality of buildings be overwhelming in a city where da Vinci would arrive, so would the vehicles: cars, buses, trains, planes, and trucks, all in one of their many forms or another.

In the roads, alleyways, and thoroughfares between the buildings of the city in this new time are what da Vinci referred to as armored carriages in countless numbers that propel themselves without the use of horses.

These carriages, too, must be fed with some type of liquid: toxic smelling, flammable liquid (the term gasoline was a 19th century term, long after da Vinci times). The parts that are not armored in metal plate are made of a strange material that is light and flexible that people call "plastic." It is a strong material and can be bent, folded, and formed in any desired shape and in various colors. This material is very popular and versatile and also used to make many other objects. (Plastic was also a 20th century discovery in the form we know today and patented then.) Da Vinci would soon learn the popularity of this material and its many, many uses in most every situation: construction, cooking, storage, and way more.

Da Vinci would see horseless carriages everywhere he looked. They were all vehicles of some sort, but he wouldn't know that word as that word evolved in the late 17th century, rooted from the Latin word that meant to carry.

They would be overwhelming but he would immediately think back right before the turn of the 16th century and remind himself of plans and sketches in one of his notebooks for a self-propelled vehicle. His idea was a wooden device on wheels that moved under its own power, not needing to be pulled by a horse or pushed in any way. This was just one of his many ideas for mechanical inventions devised for mobility, transportation, and haulage.

Looking at his sketches (Codex Atlantic), Leonardo's car wasn't designed for mass-production. It was a "cart," not what we know as a passenger car. Leonardo's contraption didn't have space for a "driver," nor a seat or sitting area of any type.

What in the world possessed Leonardo to come up with such a horseless carriage, let alone a robotic apparatus in a time when unmanned anything was an anomaly, let alone self-propelled?

The answer in da Vinci's case was strictly for entertainment: a classic case of da Vinci think.

In preparation for a Renaissance festival, Leonardo began sketching something that would be a special attraction while delighting children, aristocrats, and other festival goers. His goal was wonderment and amazement. He wanted something for his wealthy patrons to "show off."

He devised plans for a self-propelled, self-driving vehicle that would move through the festival on its own, including an automatic way for the vehicle to be steered. Da Vinci's self-propelled cart was the very first driverless vehicle concept. Pay attention Uber.

The unique contraption had no seat, so carrying passengers wasn't his goal. His sketches were rudimentary which was un-da Vinci like and did not show how the self-propelling component actually could or would work.

Thank goodness for the Codex Atlantic, for the idea was recorded, preserved on paper, and lasted throughout history, serving somewhat as a precursor to today's vehicles when times and technology allow for progress in this area.

Leonardo's travels from Florence to Milan were by horseback. With rest stops, horse fatigue, and the like, distances covered amounted to about 30 miles per day. Imagine da Vinci's frame of mind when he looked at today's transporters, a.k.a. cars and trucks, traveling more than this per hour. His thought-out plan of a robotic self-propelled cart truly was the foundation of what he could witness 500 years later in a fleet of vehicles, crisscrossing traffic, and long hauls thought to be the norm of present day life.

Leonardo would have been intrigued but totally perplexed and puzzled by the whole concept of gasoline combustion engines. He would be giddy with excitement as he hurried toward the first self-contained carriages/vehicles, anxious to see how they worked. He would definitely be "under the hood," inspecting, understanding, and learning. What propelled them? Were they like what he had proposed 500 years ago? Surely, he would want to analyze cars and engines further, to see if all things for the transporter were mechanical. Under the hood of a horseless carriage would be the propelling mechanism, a hunk of unknown metal and parts to da Vinci. He would see moving parts but not understand the invisible operational parts and things like internal combustion and gasoline.

He would want to be "behind the wheel," to understand and learn the operation of one of these modern transporters. He would witness "bells and whistles" for the sake of already improving upon an invention and making things easy, efficient, comfortable, and pleasing to the user/citizen. User experience would come into play here.

Leonardo would probably take anything of mechanical design entirely in his stride since many of his designs already analyzed and included things flight-related and mechanical-device related. Cars and trucks would be included here.

The questions would pervade throughout those things taken for granted today: How do you adjust the speed? How do you know where to go? What are the "rules?" How do you know whose turn it is to go, stop, or turn? How do you turn the vehicles on or off and is it all run on springs like Leonardo's early self-propelled cart? How do you drive? What is the effect on pedestrian flow? Do they ever run into each other? See how that curious da Vinci mind works?

If Leonardo wasn't thinking, coming up with even more questions, he would be noting, sketching, and recording. How to make it better, more efficient, and more citizen friendly would be on the top of his mind. Being dropped into today's city amongst cars, trucks, food, buildings, and people would be a true dream come true for him. Car makers today could surely use a da Vinci on staff.

DA VINCI'S MUSICAL PROWESS

Ludovico Sforza became duke in the year 1494. It was at that time that Leonardo was brought to Sforza, in Milan, to play the lute before him. Leonardo brought his own instrument which he had made himself. Yes, it was different for the time for it was mostly made of silver, in the form of a horse's head, and represented a peace offering to the Duke on behalf of Lorenzo de' Medici.

The sound quality and musical presentation, at the time of performance stood out from all the other musicians who were assembled there. The duke, hearing his delivery, became attracted to his talents to an incredible degree, and went on to commission da Vinci to paint an altarpiece of the Nativity, which he sent as a wedding present to Emperor Maximilian I of Hungary.

Da Vinci loved music. He designed not only the lute he presented to Sforza, but was involved with and designed more than a dozen musical instruments. Understanding the underlying principles of sound waves helped to produce the overall general output of the actual instrument.

Fast forward, now, to the current year. Da Vinci would experience music in so many different ways than a singular lute. He would hear multiple sounds, styles of sounds, music associated with video and live dance performance, and so much more. Music is a huge business and he would wonder how to couple that with pageant production, celebrations, banquets, and receptions for royalties. He would find that there would be so many more outlets and opportunities. This is one area where Da Vinci's connection principles would really come to the forefront and really produce.

PART IV

TECHNOLOGY

Over time, technology has revolutionized and transformed our world and daily lives in many ways. Technology has created remarkable tools and resources, especially putting useful information right in front of our eyes in many ways. Today's technology has paved the way for multi-functional devices like the smart phone, video, and computer. Computers are progressively faster, more portable, and very powerful. With all of these revolutions, technology has made our lives easier, better organized, and more entertaining, all of what da Vinci continually thought about as he kept trying for the next best innovation, concept, or idea.

There are so many new technologies that make it seem overwhelming to accept and use, whether you step here from 500 years ago or within the past year. The resounding theme with all of technology is that new technology is designed in some way, somehow, to make life better (assuming faster and cheaper would be better), a primary da Vinci principle.

Technology, or at least how da Vinci defined it during his time, was no strange concept to him. If you look at the basic definition of technology, Wikipedia states that:

> *"Technology can be most broadly defined as the entities, both material and immaterial, created by the application of mental and physical effort in order to achieve some value. In this usage, technology refers to tools and machines that may be used to solve real-world problems."*

Just looking at this definition portrays the basic premise of just about all that da Vinci was involved in and all of his accomplishments and output.

Although he was no stranger to early technology, it was crude by today's standards. Da Vinci came close to what would be considered technology in his time.

Leonardo's Codex Madrid I can be called the first and most complete treatise in the history of Renaissance mechanics and technology. Codex Madrid I provides the most comprehensive and most consistent explanation of practical and theoretical mechanics of its day.

In the Codex, there are drawings and sketches of a gear-driven calculating machine. Unfortunately, that's all it was—drawings and sketches—as it never was constructed nor completed. There are many, many more examples of drawings, sketches, and unfinished work. This concept, however, was an early foray into "technology."

This was not bits and bytes technology, but it did hold true to the Wikipedia definition of "…entities created by the application of mental and physical effort in order to achieve some value that may be used to solve real-world problems."

There is no doubt that anyone stepping into a city today, whether it be da Vinci or someone from this era, would surely be inundated by technology; some of it very visible and captivating to the eye/mind and some of it behind the scenes to make possible what is seen and used today.

No one can be sure if da Vinci even knew of the word "technology," but if he didn't, he would surely like the way future linguists would define it: the application of scientific knowledge for practical purposes. While we think of it as more modern and high-tech oriented, this definition, too, covers much of what da Vinci's life was all about.

For now, we will concentrate on the modern-day definition of technology and its connotations.

Since his time, you can say that technology has been the next revolution. The effect on our lives, the tools created, the resources available, and the accessibility of any and all information at our fingertips is only the tip of the technology iceberg. There is so much technology that makes things go and makes technology real that aren't even seen by the naked eye, da Vinci's or otherwise, regardless of the period of time.

Immediately, the apparent technology visible to a visitor to these new times would be the likes of computers, smart phones, electronic devices of all sorts, and video, all in full view and in full use. The behind the scenes technology relates to the speed of devices, the connectivity, and the tools and applications available, the quality of displays and sound, all for pleasure, communication, efficiency, and a better way of doing things.

Blink for a second. Take that one snapshot upon landing in a city. What technology do you immediately see? Apparent and in full view would be:

- Lights—basic and advanced
- Smart phones
- Video devices—television, iPads, computer screens, electronic games and books
- Food preparation and the related machinery; food delivery
- Music players, loud speakers, origination sources
- Computers
- Apps galore
- Medical technology
- Art, creation and design technology

♦ Other communication devices
   and mechanisms

There are more, but this is the snapshot. This is your blink. Think back to the definition earlier described. This would be the hottest of hotbeds for anyone with a curious mind, resulting in question after question, solution after solution, connection after connection (ideas/concepts, not electronic connections) and branching out into endless directions. There is so much along the way to learn, keep track of and to adapt, all at overwhelm speed, all with a goal to make life better. Da Vinci would be overwhelmed. See if you could list it all and keep track of it.

What other digital age exploits would he be interested in, curious about, and pursuing? There is no doubt, da Vinci would be doing something with images, more than still pictures once he found out about moving pictures/video. Add to this the whole world of Artificial Intelligence and you have a Renaissance man for the digital age. Chances are, with the affiliation of all this technology to art, he would drift towards this as his primary interest and future pursuit.

Television, video screens and displays—all very visual inventions—would be evident and in full view. Radio or other sound-generating devices would have music and voices but no pictures. Once again, he would want to dive in and see how these worked. Slicing open an electronic device would show him even more of something not comprehensible to someone from his time. The behind-the-scenes technology would be in the form of radio waves, electricity, transistors, resistors, and the like, not invented or conceived of yet in Renaissance times. He would be very frustrated at his inability to comprehend the internal design behind the devices, radio, TV, computers, smart phones, video displays or otherwise.

Let's look at the technology behemoth that we all know as communication.

Communication now is faster and more convenient, not even comparable to anything in Renaissance times. Da Vinci would be blown away and almost would not even know where to start, how to start processing or thinking, what to start tinkering with, how to even make connections with other ideas and concepts, let alone the many, many questions he would be dying to ask, even just to understand.

Thinking back, communication for da Vinci and most popular during the Renaissance, was centered around the printing press. The printing press presented an opportunity for people to share ideas, communicate, and express themselves more often and more efficiently in widespread fashion. Before that, and what da Vinci was familiar with, was letter writing. Imagine seeing this new world of technology and its many applications all replacing and supplementing the simple letter writing of yesteryear.

"The demand for perfect reproductions of texts and the renewed focus on studying them helped trigger one of the biggest discoveries in the whole of human history: printing with movable type. For me, this is the easiest and single greatest development of the Renaissance and allowed modern culture to develop," as reported by U.K.-based historian and writer Robert Wilde.

The printing press was developed in Europe by Johannes Gutenberg in 1440. It allowed Bibles, secular books, printed music, and more to be made in larger amounts and reach more people.

The progress of technology, whether during current times or da Vinci's time, has made communication incredibly fast and convenient. Just look back and see how much easier communication has become over the years. Communication tools offer one of the most significant examples of how quickly technology has evolved over the past 500 years since da Vinci's death.

To connect with someone in society today, you have many more efficient options at your fingertips, thanks to technology. You can send them a message on social media, text them on a smart phone or other electronic device, video chat, email, or put a call through on a smart phone or even a computer.

Much of present day technology is held together by the Internet.

Da Vinci would learn or at least hear about the fact that the amount of active web/Internet users globally was almost half of the world's population. He would be mesmerized by this but would have no idea what the world's population was, not to mention half of that number.

Da Vinci would fall in love with the Internet. Just look at all he did that could now be replaced and made more efficient with technology. His thoughts would revolve around all the possibilities, much the way he looked at a waterfall, the way it landed, and the swirls that resulted. As for computers, he would probably invent his own with more functions and inventiveness. His strong attraction, today, would be because of how much he liked the very different tools could help him further ideas. The whole Internet, computer and digital world would be a tool used towards his creations, to completion or never-ending. Being witness to this in today's times would satisfy him immensely and he would appreciate creation after creation from these tools.

The Internet is to our age what the printing press was to da Vinci's time. That was his way to get information more quickly, comparatively speaking, about all that he was interested in. The sharing of information would take on a whole new magnitude. Da Vinci, being a humanist at heart, would see the sharing of information as positive engagement. This positive engagement would contribute to the health and well-being of others and would endear him/them in a two-way trust that would make the citizens feel good about the times. The spreading of information also allowed people to share ideas, communicate about all sorts of things, and express themselves for their own causes and others, more often and more efficiently. Ask anyone in Renaissance times how all this communication happened for them, in the best way, and the answer predominantly would be centered around the printing press.

Fast forward 500 years. He would love the quick access to volumes and volumes of information and the instantaneous nature of obtaining it.

Watching today's people walking by, sitting and working, socializing and generally living, da Vinci would see and be amazed by things that we take for granted:

+ Weather forecasting and the ability to monitor conditions

+ Simple communication (email, texting, websites, phone calls)

+ Electronic list making—Really? Electronic Notebooks/Codices for da Vinci?

+ Trading of money online

+ Making purchases without leaving your seat

+ The answers to almost any question and research on devices in someone's hand or on a desktop.

+ Art and graphic design

+ GPS

- Text creation
- Collecting and sharing photographs

As far as this last item, da Vinci never envisioned the whole concept of photographs, but he was most intrigued by anything relating to optics and the science behind how the human eye works. He didn't comprehend photographs during his time, but he did envision, in his study of optics and the eye, a mechanism to help with those studies, that serves as the precursor for the camera. This device was known as the camera obscura. Da Vinci used this to study in depth how vision works, how light reacts, and the laws of geometric perspective. He studied that in depth to see how all that related to painting techniques.

Leonardo da Vinci wrote about and drew hundreds of diagrams of the camera obscura in his "Codex Atlanticus." This particular Codex is a twelve-volume, bound set of drawings and writings by da Vinci. It is his largest Codex. Its name comes from the fact that the large paper used to preserve original Leonardo notebook pages, were bound with the same sized paper that was used for making atlases. Codex Atlanticus contains 1,119 pages dating from 1478 to 1519, the contents covering a great variety of subjects, from flight to weaponry, with notes and sketches related to musical instruments, mathematics and botany, along with many other da Vinci notes and to-do lists.

Da Vinci was not the originator of the device described in Codex Atanticus, but he was first to notice the similarities between the way a camera obscura worked and the way the human eye and optics in general, functioned.

A camera obscura is described, according to da Vinci in his notebooks, as a dark box with a very small hole in one wall that lets in light. Directly across from the hole, the image from the outside world will be projected onto the wall upside down.

In spite of being called a camera, a camera obscura isn't really the kind of camera as we know today; it has no ability to take a photo that we can put in a frame.

Stepping into today's world, he would see photographs in frames and wonder how "past" images were captured and retained. This, along with his work in set design and festival production, would propel him to further take interest and investigate all things related to imagery—moving or static. Then he would see smart phones taking pictures and almost bypass the whole camera scene.

Da Vinci would love and fit in with Hollywood movie production. From special effects to costuming, he would love to see the production of dance numbers, general entertainment, and those events and spectacles that stood out like the productions he attempted for his aristocratic patrons in Renaissance times.

As a military engineer for Cesare Borgia, he created numerous maps that were accurate and helpful in

Cesare's war efforts. The whole concept of maps was new in da Vinci's era and would carry forward in time as maps became prolific in everyday life, navigation, and in the military. Imagine Leonardo's observation and astonishment of anything GPS-related today. Not only do you have the mapping concept and technology, but the introduction of the electronic satellite component, something that may even be too much for today's non-technology mindsets, but not da Vinci.

Da Vinci would have invented his own computer, to his liking and it would have been astounding. More functional than Microsoft, more stylish than Apple, more ingenious than the two combined. Whatever this would turn out to be, the most fitting brand identity for it would be the da Vinci Computer. Look out Apple and Microsoft.

Because of da Vinci's question-asking notions and prowess, he would very much want to question all that he saw on the Internet. His desire for experimentation to prove or disprove concepts, what he heard and saw informationally, would still be at the forefront of his thinking and analysis. He truly would not have enough hours in a day to experiment, read, sketch, develop, rinse and repeat.

Da Vinci would like so many different things that could serve as a tool that would help him to develop new ideas and connections. Digital processing and art, as in any other form of art, would be a tool. He would enjoy digital tinkering and exploring a lot, as he was ahead of his time in so many areas. He would appreciate the new output that would be a result.

Da Vinci would be quick to note that there are so many technologies to keep track of. Overwhelm is an understatement. One thing he would notice and that might help that mindset is that all of the technologies he observed were designed in one fashion or another to make life easier, more productive, efficient, and more enjoyable. That was the same as his thinking when he innovated and invented during his times. Technology would help him compile as well as stay organized with priority and results.

These could definitely be entered into a da Vinci notebook as a checklist, things observed or experienced, and items to connect and consider change for. Imagine doing it all electronically; da Vinci electronic notebooks has a nice ring to it. Da Vinci would think so, too.

A few da Vinci comments and observations about technology, so far, at this point:

It seems that computers are an essential part of everyone's life. Thanks to computers, man was able to travel in space, medical treatment and research became a reality, and the entertainment industry has taken on a life of its own. Da Vinci would love to have a computer for the pageants and celebrations that he produced, adding art to entertainment.

Every time technology is observed by da Vinci or someone else or even someone new, smart phones, mobile phones, connected devices come into play. Today he would see these devices able to do most anything a human could do, but faster and more efficiently with much greater capacity. With his curious mind, the access to information that computers, these devices, and the world wide web/Internet offer would keep his curiosity satisfied and fulfilled for eons for every question he could come up with.

Televisions, video displays of all sorts are parts of the interior and exterior landscapes all around, even in color with phenomenal sound and music.

Shifting gears a bit but still being technologically-oriented, food preparation was in full view. He observed that some food preparation is similar to his times with open flames and ovens, but add to this the microwave oven. Talk about something easier, more efficient and faster for the average citizen. Microwave ovens are that.

There is more but this perspective would be forever ingrained in the mind of this Renaissance man.

With all this talk of technology and the New World, it's almost hard for those in the New World to imagine how they ever got along without technological things. Modern technology makes you forget how you ever existed without it. Yes, you can call that technology taken for granted.

This technology spoken of here or in Renaissance times and since, has fundamentally altered the course of life in almost every area of the planet. That would be the one primary clear point da Vinci would take away from this visit.

These life alterations were all related to saving time, saving money, and enjoying life (entertainment and experiences), all in da Vinci-like fashion of making the world a better place for those that live here.

It seems for every breakthrough that has happened over time that there is more technology coming still, almost daily, with the same promise: making our lives healthier, more organized, more convenient, and more fun. Da Vinci would observe more connections than ever before as that is how new ideas are spurred.

The dawn of modern times promises more amazing developments in the world of technology. Da Vinci could see computers and applications in operation, air travel above, electronic tools for information access and communication, with nearly everything and everyone going digital in some form or another. Add to this things like medical technology, and our own human boundaries of who and what we are, will be tested.

Da Vinci would think, at first sight, that much of this technology was something of fiction. What he viewed as fiction is today commonplace and used almost on a daily basis. Technology truly does run our lives.

Reviewing the list of things that exist today that didn't in Renaissance times outlines these taken for granted, technology-related items that he would see and experience. Here is that list:

- Internet
- Television

- Radio
- Video
- Electricity
- Light/lamps
- Cars and Other Vehicles
- Pavement
- Microwave Ovens
- Phones
- Computers
- Food choices
- Sporting goods/games
- Automation
- Conveyors
- Building Equipment
- Airplanes/Air Travel
- Medical Treatment and Care
- Medicines
- Paper
- Music
- Movies
- Kitchen/Home Appliances
- Running Water
- Toilets

- Full Color Printing
- Grocery Stores
- Other Retail Shops
- Restaurants/Bars
- Time Measurement
- Bicycles, Skateboards, Roller Blades
- Soap/Detergent
- Weapons
- Plastic
- Longer Lifetimes/Expectancy
- Internal Combustion Engines
- Air Conditioner
- Furnaces
- Fuel
- Safe Drinking Water

It is probably very true that if Leonardo lived in the 21st century, he'd have his mind trained on ideas, concepts, and applications that would anticipate technology many, many years into the future.

To da Vinci, it would be clear (albeit overwhelming) that technology today would be at the forefront, would win out over all other interests, complement his thinking of other subjects, and dominate his genius mind.

COMMUNICATION

Since the beginning of time, communication has been all around. Most past communication started as and has been of a visual nature.

Volumes upon volumes are written, read, and studied regarding the basic concept of communication. Today, many take the concept for granted but walking the planet as a new first time visitor, 500 years later, da Vinci would not take it for granted. Communication enables people to share ideas, express their feelings, and contribute to discussions and debates, much like in the days of da Vinci and the Renaissance.

The basic premise of communication has not changed, but the methods and volume have changed considerably. That would be evident with one city walk-around. Communication in current times is more social and more technical, however it is still a way for people to share ideas, express feelings and opinions, learn, discuss, debate, and a way to help get things done. Looking around would reveal communication mechanisms in the form of lights, video, signage, conversations, technological devices, symbols, non-verbal mechanisms and more to study and understand; mind blowing to the new visitor and so superb compared to the inefficient and cumbersome ways of old.

Da Vinci would be witness to communication that depended on electricity, the Internet, the phone, printed media, speakers with music and video devices of one form or another, all things he didn't even know the names of or the conversational language of, not to mention the common workings of. Welcome to the New World.

Besides the overwhelm, the curiosity, and the pure excitement, immediate comparisons and contrasts would happen. As we think about his observations 500 years after his death, let's look at Renaissance communication for a comparative base.

While da Vinci couldn't know it at the time, , he lived in an era called the Renaissance period. Just like any other period of time in history, and back to that of the dawn of time, communication has been a significant part of everyday life: communication for different purposes in many different ways, to say the least.

Back in the Renaissance, the need for communication was a bit different than the need today. This certainly would be evident 500 years into the future. People normally would communicate to those in nearby towns and villages for general assistance, for the trading of goods and services, and to keep in touch with relatives about family matters. Most families lived relatively close together in this time and communication would happen easily face to face. Da Vinci would use this as his comparative base and see how all of it could be done in different ways in this new time.

The need for more urgent communication in most cases was not necessary for most, but it was for those in upper classes, (royalty, popes, statesmen and others) involved in important business, political matters, and things related to country and church management.

Contrast this to what da Vinci would see before his eyes, today. The speed of communication would be more than 10 times what he conceptualized back then.

The Renaissance was all about the visual. Things were made to be seen, which made the times and the visual communication ideal for communicating political, social, and religious messages. Early on, buildings and wall/ceiling mural paintings were sponsored by the elite, churches, guilds, and royalty. These frescoes were usually on full display for all to see and many times with a central communicative theme around them; it was very visual communication for the masses to see.

Looking at today's visual communication, it would be hard for a new visitor to detect a theme, a cause, a mission, or something sponsored as they knew it in Renaissance times. This is due to the volume and types of communication all around.

Beyond the visual landscape, communication, information, and ideas were spread mostly verbally, in face-to-face communication, by traveling merchants that moved from region to region. Anything like this, verbally communicated to more than one person, of course, was probably not as accurate as the sender wanted. Think about the childhood game of "Telephone." Information could be corrupted by indirect or inaccurate communication or interpretation, person to person.

Universities and places of study were also places where new ideas had a chance to be communicated, discussed, debated, and accepted (or not). This was the case in many universities all over Europe during this time, all known as hotbeds of communication.

Early on, there were also books. They were typically made of parchment sheets tied together. They were also extremely expensive because each copy was handwritten. Copying a Bible in this manner, could take a full year.

Behold, there was much news to communicate, during this time, whether it was the Medicis' rise to political power in Florence or popes directing armies to take over cities and regions in all of Italy. There was much to communicate about. Information about art, culture and all those involved with their output was also part of efforts to communicate on an ongoing basis. During this time in Renaissance Europe there began a communications revolution. Communication took a giant step forward with the development of the printing press. Communication centered around it providing a way in which people could share ideas, communicate, and express themselves more often and more efficiently.

Before that, however, methods of communication were very limited. Da Vinci would witness, in his new world, things that he didn't fathom, know the names of, or things that he would have no idea as to how they all worked in the world of communication. This included television, telephones, radio, Internet, all the related video screens and devices, signage, or even the postal service.

The Renaissance was an era of letter sending, inspiring many to read, write, and send more letters as an essential part of their lives and communications. In his day, communication took place in the form of corresponding by letters delivered by private messengers.

The letter was the single most literary and tactile form of communication. It was considered the glue that held society together. Letters were the connectors tying people, regions and countries together. This mechanism was in place for many years, influencing and informing people over long and even short distances, for many, many purposes.

Da Vinci wrote letters. He knew this method of communication. He would still see this in current times but wonder how letters were delivered if there were so many.

During times where communication was needed covertly, definitely needed and monumental in nature, such as during war times, communication and messages were often sent in some type of coded letter and probably hidden on a person acting as a messenger who would act in secret. It was not uncommon that information was cloaked and hidden in clothing, a walking cane, backpack or even in a messenger's shoes, stockings or the garb of the day.

Many people in da Vinci's area during his time were illiterate, which meant that writing a letter by themselves was almost impossible. If they did construct one, they would have to consider that the letter's recipient would likely have been unable to read it on his or her own. Messages, then, would have often been oral communications, totally dependent on the messenger.

After letter writers finished, the letter would be folded and sealed with sealing wax, leaving an imprint of a seal of significance, sometimes a family crest, symbol of business, or something of a personal nature. On the front side of the letter, the name of the recipient, a location, if known, and general indications how to find this person, would be written.

The letter was then ready to be sent. The elite and rich would employ a personal courier or a courier that was going in the same intended direction carrying letters for others. This person could be a monk, a clergyman, a merchant, a government agent, banker, or any random traveler.

Da Vinci would wonder where the letter writers were in new times. He soon would learn that technology had largely taken over this form of communication, not quite replacing it.

The postal service as we understand it today, centralized and available for any member of the society, did not exist then. There was no need for one because, generally, only the upper part of society and guilds would send or receive letters.

Imagine these problems related to couriers/ letters and communication in Renaissance times:

- ◆ The courier is leaving and no one is sure when the next one will appear and travel in the intended direction.

- ◆ There is a delay because no one would be headed to the intended destination.

- ◆ Horses were unavailable and needed proper rest to make a letter-sending journey.

- ◆ As compared to problems often heard of today:

- ◆ The Internet is down

- ◆ I didn't have a strong phone signal

- The information is in another file (electronic)
- I'm out of charge

Everybody who travelled could become a courier. Many could earn some additional income to cover travel expenses by picking up a few letters to transport.

Letter writing, even in da Vinci's time and even for him, was not as easy as it is today. In fact, it was a bit cumbersome and sometimes inefficient. Imagine da Vinci learning about the current postal system and email to replace the crude methods of letter writing and communication of old times. He would gladly resort to the technology that overtook letter writing.

Leonardo was a lifelong, continuous learner whose many interests led him to pursue learning in multiple ways. Da Vinci relied on direct experience for much of what he did. This plus written sources and the communication of these supported his theories, methods, and inventions. Many times, the written sources were in the form of books, much like supporting communication today.

Leonardo was a tireless and inquisitive reader. He owned more than 200 books about science, technology, literary and religious topics—a lot of books for someone of his time. He was an avid reader, he had books on a wide variety of subjects, like The Holy Bible, books about surgery, *The Divine*

Comedy by Dante, Ovid's *Metamorphoses*, books about mathematics, geometry, and astronomy among others.

Libraries, especially as known today, were few, far between, and small. The Library of the Dominican Convent of San Marco, in Florence, is known as the First "Public" Library in Renaissance Europe. Under Lorenzo il Magnifico of the famous Medici family, the library became one of the most frequented and favorite meeting places for Florentine humanists, for it was here that they could access the magnificent book collections assembled by the Medici family, which included rare Greek and Latin texts. Leonardo would surely be seeking a meeting place of the same sort with similar collections. He would find them in abundance and visit in total disbelief. The collections, the titles, the volumes, the accessibility was always something he dreamed of during his book collecting days. Wouldn't he love to be introduced to Amazon's Kindle?

Da Vinci was widely read. He read as many books as he could find or borrow. Once the printed book form was introduced to him, he became deeply curious of this one great invention of Renaissance times. He knew, once he saw it, what would happen to communication. Other written communication in the form of manuscripts, notes, sketches, and printed books played a key role in all of his research aiding in the resulting formation of ideas, thoughts, theories, and approaches of all that he worked on and took interest in.

Another "OMG" moment for da Vinci and his visit would be a trip to a bookstore or library. His mind would be blown. He would freak out, to put his observational status in present day terminology. He would want to inspect the covers, the material, the paper, treating all as treasures. He would flip pages and assuming a way around the language barrier, he would jump from title to title to title. He truly would want to know about all subjects.

The libraries of current times would prove to be unending playgrounds for da Vinci; so much so that he may have to revisit his sleeping habits and patterns as he would want to stay awake in pursuit of these new-found treasures. There was just so much to see, discover, absorb, and use when connecting ideas, comparing concepts, and learning all that was offered.

The culture of the Renaissance was focused on communication. It was no wonder that the invention of the printing press happened. The printing press allowed the spread of culture and knowledge through the beginning two centuries of Renaissance times. It really did change the story of the rebirthing of new times. The printing press changed communication by allowing books to be printed faster, allowing ideas, such as Protestantism, to spread quickly, while allowing people, in general, to learn more about many things.

The introduction of the printing press is widely regarded as the single most important event of the second millennium, and is one of the significant, defining moments of the Renaissance. Much has been written about the invention of the printing press and the effect on the world, then and now. Here, we will leave thoughts related to da Vinci's observation of technology and leave the volumes written about the printing press as supplemental information for you.

Individuals who wish to be on the frontier of change head to dynamic places in search of like-minded innovators and stimulating ideas using published and distributed information to establish their footholds. Communication with and through books would do this. The same would be seen in places today like Silicon Valley and other technological, innovative, and modern hotbeds of progressiveness. Florence during the Renaissance was similarly attractive. Florence also was a melting pot of those that contributed ideas, techniques, and information that helped to define the art movement synonymous with The Renaissance.

Walking present day Earth, communication would be so abundant, one couldn't tell what was communication or not, as communication is defined then and now as the imparting or exchanging of information or news. Regardless, it was part of a new world: one that da Vinci had not envisioned; one that he would want his hands on to do more research, spread more ideas, and make things better, a common theme in all that he did.

THE INTERNET

As da Vinci moved around and observed, experienced, and learned, he eventually would come across the Internet. He would learn about electricity, radio waves, cellular technology, television, and general electronic connectivity. The sequence of his observing and learning in this case is unknown as it would be a lot to understand 500 years later. There are even people in current times that struggle with the simple understanding of the same. Their observing and learning can't be defined either.

Let's make the assumption that he would learn about the Internet. Now the question remains how would he adapt it to everyday life? How is it adapted to everyday life now and what parts would he integrate and connect (non-electronic connection)?

There is no question, whether for da Vinci or everyday people of this time that the Internet has turned our daily lives upside down. Nothing since the printing press has revolutionized communications like the Internet has. The Internet affects all parts of everyday life from entertainment, obtaining information, purchasing goods and services, or communicating with friends and family, not to mention the plethora of business applications.

Reading on the Internet has partially and maybe, for some people, mostly replaced books and newspapers. Of course, daily newspapers were a thing new to da Vinci in the first place. Now some of these things, new to him, would be surpassed with more technology and more advancements. There was so much technological development in the past 500 years that he could skip over much of it to get to today's technology point.

Da Vinci would research and scour online to see instantaneous information related to anything he was working on, studying, or thinking about for the future. The immense quantities of information are literally in endless supply almost about any subject under the sun. Content not only is supplied by authorities, universities, and researchers but also shared by everyday users, friends, family, associates, acquaintances, famous people, and more. Figuring out all this for a fresh centuries-later visitor is unfathomable so it will be left at that for the assumption of the visit.

On top of all this is the whole creation side of life that da Vinci was well versed in and more in tune with. Seeing how creation could happen with these new modern tools would turn him into a master creator on steroids.

Telling others of his discoveries, asking questions of items that were puzzling or unknown would be two of the things taken for granted today, that happen with e-mail and electronic communication (websites, online recordings, and video).

Da Vinci would be witness to societal change, past and present. What was once the Renaissance era, then the Industrial Age, has become a networked information age, not all before his eyes as he is seeing it 500 years later. A lot happens in that kind of time frame. It truly has become a societal evolution of mankind.

The next stage of all of this is portable, mobile, instant communication and exchange. Those black devices he first witnessed that people were talking into would be the pulse of everyday life. This has happened on a personal level within the structure of society. It is now, in current times, possible for communication with an unending amount of people, freely, easily, and without restriction.

All he could think about was the opportunity and power of creativity and how it could improve everyone's life, a very noble cause that he always had at the forefront of all he did.

Da Vinci would see this opportunity now and for the future. He clearly would be witness to the fact that the future of the Internet had just begun.

Leonardo was also a philosopher. He pontificated about past times and future times. It almost looks like he had the Internet in mind during some of his philosophical dissertations.

Da Vinci said, "Everything connects to everything else." That, alone, could be the basis of a business plan and model for Apple, Microsoft or any of the electronic/technology connectors. These connections would serve as his "Internet base," as he observed, learned and applied with his new-found tools and knowledge, Internet related.

PART V

ART

"I must depict this scene [Last Supper] as though I were present in the room and the retina of my eye held for a brief moment all that was before it as though frozen in time."

-Leonardo da Vinci

Da Vinci was an artist. This is the subject of many, many books and chapters within art-related books, da Vinci-related, and more.

Let's look at what most people think da Vinci is famous for, art, and how that would influence his observations today. Background here lends so much perspective to bring Renaissance life forward joining with Leonardo da Vinci's present day observations. You are learning that in present day, and so is da Vinci.

There is no doubt by now that Leonardo's art was influenced and immersed with his understanding of science.

During the Renaissance period, many aspiring artists painted religious scenes, portraits of religious icons, and related religious subjects. Many were sponsored by the Church itself or patrons of the Catholic Church and Christianity. In addition, many of these artists were often commissioned to use their talents to decorate the interiors of churches. Just look at what Michelangelo did for Pope Julius II on the ceiling of the Sistine Chapel. Leonardo was commissioned by Ludovico Sforza, the Duke of Milan to paint the Last Supper on the walls of the refectory of the Convent of Santa Maria delle Grazie in Milan, Italy.

Da Vinci would wonder if this type of patronage existed today. There are many, many paintings, religious and otherwise, in present day times. Who commissioned these? Were there primarily a few artists or many? Were they painted by craftsmen and true masterpiece artists? Looking at the magnitude of everything, many different types of painters and paintings would be the most logical answer to the same question for all topics.

Portraits of everyday citizens were still a new development at the time of the Mona Lisa painting. Normally, artists would produce pieces depicting kings, the elite, other royalty, aristocrats or clerics. Having one's portrait painted simply because one could afford it, and wanted it, was a novelty of the time. A commission today, would still have to come from someone, but it could have been a person, company, or organization. Artists didn't paint for free, typically, unless it was in their apprentice studio or for their own practice.

The idea that the Renaissance was a rebirth or rediscovery is best exemplified by how artists, like da Vinci, used the works of ancient Greece and Rome as their foundation, whether it be painting or sculpting. Works consisted of the use of stone, bronze, and paint and turned out to be some of the greatest of artistic feats. Many of the concepts of artistic beauty that Leonardo would lay eyes on in modern times are, in some ways, defined by the achievements of Renaissance master painters. Depending on where he saw art displayed, much of it would look familiar to a degree, especially with the influence presented by the Catholic Church. But much would be new, abstract, exotic, totally unfamiliar, and totally unrelated to the Church.

Art in the Renaissance era reflected the times. Paintings gained depth and detail; realistic backgrounds carried the eye beyond the subject in the foreground. That characteristic showed up in the Mona Lisa, but it isn't talked about as much as her smile and eyes. Leonardo da Vinci was a pioneer of this perspective, due to his reading and studying of the art and architectural work of the Ancient Greeks. This knowledge drove his work. This continues to today's time where his art and architecture still shows up.

Da Vinci would walk around today and see churches, but oh how different they appeared. Many would be built and shaped in contemporary style, not resembling the gothic architecture of old. Da Vinci would observe exteriors made of gray, cold concrete with small windows. He would see circular style churches. Many would be colorless. Many seemed like they had nothing to do with religious tones of yesteryear, almost a disconnect to all that da Vinci once saw. It would cause him to re-think commissioning and patronage, in addition to the overall influence of the Church.

Da Vinci's stature as an artist was great because of his highest quality output and the fact that artists were at the top of society during the Renaissance. Being a patron to a leading artist like da Vinci was very trendy then; not as much in today's time. Today, it is more about production than craft.

Da Vinci was a problem solver applying that approach in many fields. He would not necessarily approach things as an artist first. He did, however, bring the sensibility of an artist and designer to all he did especially when meeting up with scientific concepts and thinking.

By now, you know that da Vinci was viewed by others and himself as an engineer, architect, and a painter. Renaissance pundits argued that art should be elevated to the levels of theory, poetry, the lessons of the Greeks and Romans, and historical writing. Leonardo supported and extended this by linking art to the science of optics that he studied unendingly, in addition to nature and the mathematics of perspective and proportion. Leonardo's argument was that creativity is the combination of observation with imagination; reality of what is versus what could be. The best painters could show and illustrate that. What better platform to observe and think "what could be" than present day times and surroundings, whether by painting, inventing, observing, writing and sketching, or other endeavor.

The science of optics and human sight has been mentioned. Da Vinci's curiosity of human sight centered around his premise that it was the superior sense. In Codex Ash he stated, "The eye, which is said to be the window of the soul, is the principal means by which the brain's sensory receptor may fully and magnificently contemplate the infinite works of nature." It is needless to say how much the eye and optical senses would be at work on a visit to current times.

Leonardo based knowledge on actual experiences and demonstration. He can say that he liked fantasy but fantasy, even though he might not have used that word, was really "what could be." Taking what he knew and "what could be" over 500 years ago, his masterpieces were painted. He would carry this notion through to observations in these new times for him. He could look at moving cars, tall buildings, people bustling about, walls, skies, landscapes, food, and start to imagine what could be. He would think back to his Renaissance days and the many thoughts related to what could be and witness some of those 500 years later.

Just consider what he would see today, art with a taste of architecture or architecture with a taste of art... either or both with a side of science:

- Curved entrances and doorways
- Cubism—early 20th century architecture, but da Vinci knew of this concept before its time
- Classical architecture that was the root of Renaissance architecture stemming from ancient Greek architecture
- Multiple piece buildings
- Focus on physical structures
- Emphasis on materials and functionality
- Technology influence past, present, and future
- Building ornamentation and detail

Leonardo's paintings weaved together light, shadows, colors, perspective, proportion, movement, emotion all with detail galore and with scientific influences. He worked on all of these, along with the study of human anatomy to perfect his paintings, all in an effort to treat art as a science. A good example of this and his level of detail is the mere painting of Mona Lisa's lips. Some say it took four years, some say eight, and others say it took 12 years to complete the lips on this famous painting. It is known today that experts at the Louvre Museum in Paris, France have verified that it took a long time, probably closer to 12 years to capture the air of mystery in her smile. He continually was revising and adding finer and finer brush strokes to get his talent to match his vision, what could be. Leonardo excelled here in combining motion and emotion as a result of his scientific studies of facial muscles and other human anatomy.

He would walk around today staring at mouths, expressions, facial muscle lineage, and more all because of his perspective of combining art and science. Da Vinci was known to spend an inordinate amount of time watching people so he could capture their expressions to then be sketched in his notebooks. He would study the subject in detail and sketch expressions, whole heads, partial views, and more, all related to the face and its movement. With people in new times, he could get plenty of expressions to study and sketch, but add to that hair styles, clothing, make-up, jewelry, and the whole persona would fulfill his people-observation desires, more so than in Renaissance times.

Just envision the following: "I must depict this scene [Last Supper] as though I were present in the room and the retina of my eye held for a brief moment all that was before it as though frozen in time."

You can bet that his new notebooks, full of notes, sketches and observations, from his current visit would be overflowing. That retina would not have enough capacity for all that was before it, during this time.

Volumes upon volumes have been written about da Vinci's art and science but when you really break it down, drawing was, for da Vinci, primarily a learning exercise: a type of brainstorming on paper.

In the words of da Vinci himself, "The eye does not know the edge of anybody." This was another way to say, "remove the limitations; let your imagination run" and in present day vernacular, get out of the box.

In her 2015 commencement address to the Southern Vermont College graduating class, Dr. Karen Gross, Contributor—Huffington Post and Former President, Southern Vermont College; Former Senior Policy Advisor, US Department of Education, urged graduates to color outside of the lines much in support of and along the same lines as da Vinci's quote on removing limitations and letting imaginations run:

> *"Color with joy and with creativity. Let your crayons go wherever they want to go.*
>
> *And, if possible and appropriate, feel the freedom to discard the pre-prepared drawings we are given in life and make your own drawings.*

Be Bold; Use Bright Colors; Design Your Future;
Color Freely In, and Outside the Lines."

Da Vinci observed a very colorful world before him, colorful as in colors everywhere for everything. The range of colors would be enormous, especially in the mind of someone who had to mix things together to produce color, back in his time. He would immediately ask how one could make all the mixtures. Where did all the color come from?

The real lesson da Vinci offers the world of science, mechanics, engineering, and industry is less in his actual inventions and ideas and more in his level of innovation and demonstrations as he worked through and took on another dimension of science meeting art.

SKETCHING OUT THE INDUSTRIAL AGE

Da Vinci designed things with art and mechanics in mind. His design for a file cutter shows a mechanical idea in action. A crank is turned to engage a pulley that lifts a weight. This could have been his way to sketch out the next age in mechanics or industry as he knew it, not fully realizing the connection with science, art, architecture, and engineering.

Leonardo applied his perceptual capabilities to scientific topics. He furthermore took on these artistic and engineering challenges that built on his knowledge. We've already seen Leonardo's natural state of mind was to integrate art, design, and science. Add engineering and architecture to this.

Leonardo's observations would consist of looking for science and mathematics and their relationship to perspective, proportion, patterns, shapes, and symmetries underlying art and nature.

What would he see from an artist's perspective; what would he see from a scientist's perspective; what would he see combining the two? What would his observation list look like for these perspectives, in today's times?

The application of science to art allowed da Vinci to master the look of his works. This, alone, affected the way he was looked upon by his peers and his societal circle, elevating both the practice of art and the position that the fine art of painting was still enjoying during his visit to today's times. Da Vinci would be proud. Da Vinci would be elevated—maybe even more so in current times than in Renaissance times.

ADVANCEMENT OF ART THROUGH SCIENCE IN THE NEW WORLD

Da Vinci was most interested in doing novel things in the art world, whether it was a particular emotion, finely tuned lips, a flinching appendage in the heat of battle, or a solemn smile of a mother with children. This was certainly the case when da Vinci painted the most famous of smiles in the Mona Lisa masterpiece.

Even though, da Vinci's completed paintings are limited, he would still be interested in how he was viewed in this area and what his reputation in current times was.

He would quickly learn that by one mention of his name, first, last or combined, that the first immediate thought of anyone in new times would be an association with Mona Lisa. Da Vinci would find out that the Mona Lisa painting was the best known, most viewed and visited, most written about work of art in the world, now and of all time. It would be a humbling thought, as da Vinci said on his death bed that he still needed to finish the Mona Lisa painting, even after all the years of working on it.

Da Vinci would further learn that the Mona Lisa was termed a masterpiece in today's art world and otherwise. It continues to inspire and amaze those from all over the world who come to view it. Da Vinci would be embarrassed that it hangs in its own room in a famous French museum.

Da Vinci would be familiar with museums as he knew of The Capitoline Museums in Piazza del Campidoglio in Rome, Italy. These museums hold the oldest public collection of art in the world, which began in 1471 when Pope Sixtus IV donated a group of important ancient sculptures to the people of Rome.

He would immediately want to visit other museums, understand what each museum collected and contained, and ask if it was just paintings or if there were other artifacts of interest or significance in each.

Da Vinci would learn of mystery and intrigue around the painting. He would find this comical and almost to the point of, "What's so intriguing? Just ask me why she is smiling, if she was painted on purpose to have following eyes, who she really is and anything else you are curious about." These mysteries, da Vinci would learn, have been and will be intriguing us over and over as no one has or will ever have the real answers. It is the breadth and depth of the possible interpretations of her smile and aura that make her special. She continues to be and express whatever the viewer wants, adding even more to the continuing intrigue.

When Leonardo painted his masterpiece, Mona Lisa, he was attempting something novel in the art world.

"Leonardo wanted to portray the complex psychological life of a real person," says Monsignor Timothy Verdon, who teaches art in Florence through Stanford University. "He may have wanted to see the play of different feelings and responses to different stimuli on her face. The emotions, the intelligence, the obvious wit that he captured are what makes Lisa's face so alive and so fascinating to us."

With his scientist hat on, da Vinci was able to give the Mona Lisa that mystical look and smile on her face because he had studied over and over, all the muscles in the face involved in smiling. This, more than any other study, exemplified da Vinci's approach and attitude of science supporting art.

As it turned out, that most famous smile was as much a technical achievement as it was an achievement of art. No longer was a grin a grimace. It took years of experimentation, trial and error, but he reached what would become known as a new level of technical genius long after he was gone. It did and he would be proud of this association.

He viewed The Last Supper as a performance. He stated,

> *"It seemed that my fame had spread far and wide and the painting of the Last Supper became a spectacle for all to witness when they would. Those who came stood for long periods behind me and observed what I was doing as though I was working before a time bomb detonated. We are objects of admiration depending on our performances. I obviously fared better than most because of what emerged from the flatness of the wall in the refectory of the Convent of Santa Maria delle Grazie in Milan, Italy."*

Although da Vinci wasn't there, I was one who stood for long periods observing that flatness of the wall with his beautiful art adorning it.

Whether it was something novel or, thinking back to his zeal for scientific education and the base of it all for his art, da Vinci thought many times about where and how artistic advancement through science would happen in the New World. Many things would seem "industrious" in nature, absent of "art." Many things, technology and science based, were "behind the scenes" and not touched by art. He would be dismayed, but as he continued his journey, he would find many other artistic and scientific moments, together. It deserved more exploration and more observation, especially on the science end of the spectrum.

Just a quick note to state that although he was visiting modern times, pens and pencils as they are known today would be in limited use. Electronic notation is quickly becoming more the norm but da Vinci's simple observation, especially with his love of art and sketching, of these pens and pencils would cause wonderment about these writing and drawing/sketching implements, before he ever got to electronic tools and art.

Leonardo led a movement of combining technology and art, even though his idea of technology was nothing like it is today. What he would see today would be digital platforms for viewing images, pictures and art, integrated with products, packaging, and for personal viewing. He would wonder and see it to fruition that this combination and direction would also employ more people, make more people interested in art, and elevate the craft to a new level.

SCIENCE

"To develop a complete mind: Study the science of art; Study the art of science. Learn how to see. Realize that everything connects to everything else."

-Leonardo da Vinci

In the times and occasions that da Vinci learned of his own self, it was mostly in reference to and a classification of him as a painter. He would want it known and had plenty to back it up that he was as much a scientist as he was an artist. His journey, as he reconciles this with art, continues.

Everything you read today talks about da Vinci the painter with usually a footnote or subscript of him also being an engineer and scientist. Which was he? He was all three and more, but didn't draw the line or assign the title. Maybe once in a while he would take on the title of military engineer, but it depended on his goals and objectives, interests and pursuits at the time.

To support and enhance his detailed and realistic paintings, da Vinci invested a lot of time in the study of several fields of science. He studied anatomy to better understand muscles and their arrangement within the human body. He studied physics to learn how light reflects off a subject, water movement, friction, and more. He studied chemistry to create the perfect paint mixtures as well as chemical plastic. There was much more, but these alone put him in the scientist classification.

Leonardo was obsessed with the natural world. From a young age, he was determined to reflect every detail in the world around him, in the natural world he walked in.

Da Vinci said, "Nature is the source of all true knowledge. She has her own logic, her own laws, she has no effect without cause nor invention without necessity."

As his curiosity took him in all directions, Leonardo always used a method that would become recognizable as the scientific inquiry: observation up close, testing, testing, and more testing of the observation, illustration of the subject object or phenomenon at the highest detail with thorough, explanatory notes. The results of this method were notebooks of notes, sketches, and pictures on a whole host of topics, from the nature of the sun, moon, and stars to the formation of fossils and, perhaps most notably, the mysteries of flight, light, optics, complete anatomy, physics, and engineering.

YOUNG SCIENTIST

It was under the apprenticeship of Andrea del Verrocchio in Florence, that Leonardo's appreciation of science started. He would have been about 17 at that time. He figured out how science could enhance his work as a painter. This further instigated him to learn more about various fields of science including "art related" disciplines: metalwork, the human form and anatomy, plants and animals, optics, perspective, light, and the use of color, among other disciplines.

In Verrocchio's workshop/studio, Leonardo was instructed on things like perspective, paint color and mixing, metal casting, particularly bronze, wax and clay modeling, and sculpting after that. Of course, just like jobs and workers he would view at the bottom of today's work ladder, he swept floors, manually crushed minerals and stones for color, manufactured tools of painting like easels (crude), and brushes of animal bristles. Fires would be tended to that served as the melting force of metals used for art pieces. Looking around today, he would see remedial work like this except for things related to the melting of metals. Where were the melting fires in the New World?

Verrocchio was big into sculpting and teaching sculpting. While Leonardo did some sculpting, painting took over his art world more. Walking around today he wouldn't see as many works of sculpture as he was used to seeing in his times. He wouldn't be sure Verrocchio's output would be needed or wanted; his teachings surely would be.

While there are few examples then and now of Leonardo's sculptural work, he did like the integration of motion and a three-dimensional quality that sculpting represented. The whole medium of sculpting influenced his drawing, painting, related detail, and portrayal of real life. The feeling of motion was integrated and another dimension would pop things right into a 3D rendering.

Modern sculpture takes many forms, using many different types of materials producing many types of output, some recognizable as sculpting and some not. Leonardo would have to learn these differences and similarities as he searched for familiarity in this realm.

Da Vinci continued learning about art intensively, but his interests started to branch out into these other areas. He was fortunate to be close to the river Arno. These surroundings allowed him to explore the natural sciences and provided all kinds of nature to observe, to sketch, and to study. He studied rock formations, sea shells, water flow, caves, and fossils. This was more fuel for his scientific curiosities and career.

Dr. Peter Abrahams, Professor of Clinical Anatomy at Warwick Medical School, England and visiting professor and part-time anatomy faculty with St.

George's University, credited Leonardo's ability to develop accurate renderings of the human body due to a combination of unique skill sets.

He stated,

> *"Leonardo dissected between twenty and thirty bodies himself, like any professor of anatomy would in the modern era. But he then had the ability to draw what he saw very accurately and more excitingly than that, he was able to use his knowledge of mechanics and other aspects of engineering to determine how the body worked. Da Vinci had the combination of artistic, scientific and engineering knowledge which enabled him to put it all together and understand it."*

The combination of being an artist and a scientist contributed greatly and uniquely to this approach, and his results and output.

While he would want it known that he was a scientist as much as an artist, that wasn't always his first pursuit. Nature played an important part here. His exploration of all things nature was a way for him to gain knowledge of all that the human eye could see. Art is a "snapshot" of that. Just understanding human anatomy, the workings of the muscles, how they fit with the skeleton, all served as his ambition to make art perfect or the best it could be. Understanding what underlies it, did that.

In a letter to Ludovico Sforza, the ruler of Milan, da Vinci listed his many strengths. These included mostly military engineering device design, bridge designs, moving armored tanks, tunnel engineering, and more. It wasn't until the end of the list offered, that he mentioned something to the effect of, "…and, oh by the way, I am a painter." The functional lines crisscrossed and overlapped and sometimes were non-existent, just the way he liked it.

SCIENTIFIC IMPACT

The rehabilitation and rediscovery of nature and its positive impact was one of the significant innovations of the Renaissance.

Da Vinci's impact on society was that he revolutionized scientific research. Much of da Vinci's scientific work in many fields and the whole scientific method that he followed, fueled scientists for years to come. What he would view on his current, "new times," journey would be the results of this approach consistent with his previous methods.

If he had the mathematics and accurate measuring instruments of today or even of a later date than Renaissance time, his inventions would have resulted in even more possibilities rather than doodles and sketches in his notebooks.

Da Vinci took up the diverse and varied fields of learning not to distance himself from being a painter but to lift up the craft, the techniques, and the output. Scientific learning and his studies allowed da Vinci to improve the look and detail of his works. Others followed, wanting the same uplifting of the craft.

Scientific learning allowed da Vinci to improve the detail and appearance of his paintings. This elevated artistic practice and his position as a fine art painter that we all know today.

Among all of science today, the harmony of scientific laws, and the relationship with mathematics can be seen. That's exactly what Leonardo saw then and now. Art, shapes, and perspective were all over the place in new times, so the sorting out of the mathematic and scientific law would take some time.

Da Vinci saw that the creations of the universe and the creations of man were part of one, great balanced whole, and that to understand art and to understand science were essentially the same thing. That was the essence of being both a scientist and an artist.

Science is about creativity, insight, invention, and seeing things that nobody else has seen before. Leonardo is the most creative figure in the field of science in that respect, making observations of a level of detail that no other is or was doing.

Da Vinci would see plenty of science in action upon his visit. The question was how this would be integrated into the art that he saw or even that he would want to create. The murals, the images, the portraits would be modern, not all religious, sometimes abstract in nature, and not always of people's faces.

Science that we take for granted today, would allow new observations by da Vinci:

- Food preparation and agriculture
- The effect of hot and cold systems— refrigeration and the boiling of water
- Burning of fuel
- Light by candlelight
- Running water and waste disposal
- Electronic technology and connectivity
- Vehicles and power engines
- Internal combustion
- Clothing material and textiles— variety and mass production
- Cleaning products—chemistry
- Medical technology and treatments
- …much, much more.

Would any of this affect his perspective of art and the accompanying detail and quality? It all depends on the observer, their perspective and a keen, experienced, trained eye. In this case, da Vinci. In this case, yes, it would affect perspective, art, and quality.

LIGHT AND OPTICS

One of the areas of science that he studied was light and optics. Da Vinci's hours that he spent studying color, light, shadows, nature, and the inner workings of human anatomy allowed him to create the concept bearing its Italian name, sfumato. Sfumato in Italian means smoke. His sfumato technique allowed for blurred edges and outlines blending shades, light, and color into a mellow appearance, leaving a viewer with a perspective open to their imagination.

The study of muscles and the human body affected much of da Vinci's art. Mona Lisa and her expression, mannerism, and implied motion was no exception.

Da Vinci learned that facial expression depends mainly on the acute corners of the mouth and the wider corners of the eyes. Merging into soft shadows and exploiting sfumato left open to the imagination of a viewer what mood Mona Lisa is in as she gazes back at us. Your guess is as good as the millions of views of that iconic masterpiece.

One area that da Vinci was an expert in, because of his study of light, was an art technique referred to as chiaroscuro. Chiaroscuro is the use of light and dark shades and colors to create a sense of depth and structure in a two-dimensional drawing or painting. Da Vinci was one of the first artists to focus on light in this way. That's not a surprise.

Chiaroscuro is not as evident in today's times. Other techniques are present and the reliance on shadows, light, color, and shades is not as predominant in today's visual brilliance, compared to Renaissance art.

He realized through his experimentation and deep study of light and optics, that what the naked eye sees depends on light and surroundings. He would see that in today's art, regardless of final form. He also knew that familiarity and perception played a role, but he would like what he saw here.

Botany

Another branch of science that contributed to da Vinci's scientist status and classification was botany, the study of plants. While botanists rely on their artistic skills to convey scientific ideas, da Vinci did the opposite, which was no shock. He studied plants so that he could create more accurate and more detailed art.

The art of botany changed during the Renaissance. Da Vinci was one of the masters that became celebrated for his studies of flowers and plants that depicted both plant structure and patterns, and his works are considered to be part of the first modern artistic representations of botany.

Da Vinci's sketches of plants and animals helped to prepare more studies of nature or prepare for a larger painting of some similar elements. As an example, he sketched a trio of plants. His drawing of a trio of plants is hard to classify as either an artistic undertaking or a scientific diagram, because it seems to record and investigate both scientific and artistic matters.

Da Vinci stared at trees and plants and was astonished at the basic branching of each. He then connected, as he did with many other ideas and concepts, the branching to the branching of streams, rivers, and tributaries which further was extended to his thoughts on the branching of blood vessels in human anatomy. Observing nature was continuous and ongoing wherever he could find it. He would certainly be looking for it in new times, between buildings, in open spaces and designated parks, and outside the city.

Vasari stated that Leonardo spent much of his time studying and drawing flowers and plants. He went on to state that, "A look at works like Virgin of the Rocks and The Annunciation shows that Leonardo must have expended a great deal of effort to get his paintings correct down to the last detail. Indeed, the variety of plant life in Virgin of the Rocks is nothing short of amazing."

Da Vinci learned more about anatomy, animals, and botany by drawing and sketching related items. His pursuit of science is what helped him understand the order of these. Doing this allowed his mind to make connections, answer questions, and conceptualize art on paper.

ANATOMY

Another field of science that would help create more accurate and more detailed art was anatomy. Not only da Vinci, but many Italian Renaissance artists learned anatomy as a way to improve their drawings of the human form.

Da Vinci was a leader in bringing a scientist's eye to art. A whole new book could be written about da Vinci and anatomy. For now it will just be summarily touched upon to demonstrate the relationship with art and science.

Just like botany, just like light and optics, just like other areas of science, Leonardo studied human anatomy primarily to improve his art. Renaissance artist and engineer, Leon Battista Alberti, had written that, "…anatomical study was essential for an artist because properly depicting people and animals requires beginning with an understanding of their insides."

The way to bring that science into art was to understand how the human body was constructed and how it worked. Da Vinci dove deep into understanding where emotions came from and the subsequent expression of those emotions. He dissected human cadavers, drew muscles, nerves, veins, and vessels reflecting his roles as scientist, engineer, and artist.

In da Vinci's notebooks he emphatically stated, "It is necessary for a painter to be a good anatomist, so that he may be able to design the naked parts of the human frame and know the anatomy of the sinews, nerves, bones, and muscles." Based on his lessons from Alberti, da Vinci wanted to associate, learn, and understand how psychological emotions tied into physical motions. This led to an interest in other anatomical systems and in how they related. This is reflected and perfected in his painting.

Renaissance art did not limit itself to its grandly detailed appearance. The Renaissance emphasis was a new intellectual discipline: Perspective was studied and created, light and shadow techniques were developed, and the whole of human anatomy was dissected and mapped out—all in pursuit of a new Renaissance realism capturing the beauty of the world as it really was, including motion and expressions, the humanistic approach.

At the time of the Renaissance and early modern eras, "science" did not yet exist under this name. It was predominantly a human endeavor, and the artist and scientist came to know the natural world was inseparable from the Renaissance humanist project of realizing the full extent of human potential.

In all that da Vinci did, it wasn't like he intentionally said on a given day that he was going to be a scientist and study only scientific things nor did he classify himself as an artist on a given day. He viewed them as common and almost the same mindset. He really couldn't imagine one without the other. His observations, notes, and sketches were all captured, contextually, whether art or science. That would be a tough thing to see, to explain, and to live with in today's times. Many would see benefits for cross-disciplinary learning, many would still erect boundaries between the two. According to da Vinci, the separation of the two are only labels. Da Vinci's mindset heading out into the New World was that if you want to see the world and life for what it really is, then you have to observe and live both without such boundaries and bias.

Now comes the part where he has to interpret his New World views with any scientific meaning that he was experienced in.

ARCHITECTURE

In today's world, da Vinci would see countless buildings, people bustling, technology in full view and behind the scenes, and activities of everyday life. He would recognize past influences in all that he viewed. Art, architecture, engineering, and science influenced all his views. Some of this influence was in view today and would probably continue into the future.

To reconcile, in his own mind, why architecture was important today, all he had to do was look up and all around. He was surrounded by it in the form of buildings and the designed environment. Not only buildings, but the spirit of architects who designed that environment.

Da Vinci knew that architecture was influenced by the culture of the times. There were thousands of shapes in view, transcending a line of cultures from present times to centuries back.

Old time architects will state that when learning about ancient cultures, people point first and foremost to the architecture of the time. Da Vinci would surely see new architecture, influenced by present culture, the culture of his day, and the many other cultures along the way to present times. Architecture was an expression of values, time and place, just like those old time architects pointed out.

Just looking around he would see familiar architecture:

- Arches
- Domes
- Gables
- Facades
- Angles
- Ornamentation

All of these were in clear view and used in buildings of all shapes, sizes, and types.

Da Vinci would see the make-up of today's architecture in the form of steel, wood, glass, sometimes manufactured in a mass-produced way, and sometimes crafted and customized for single applications.

He immediately would question production of the materials: Where were they made, where did the raw materials come from, who made them, what was the process, and how did this evolve into present form?

He would question, elevate his curiosity and start to piece, analyze, combine, compare, and propose more ideas thereafter.

Da Vinci's architecture was characteristic of the Renaissance era, but there was always a hint of a future focus. That's the way architects generally think. His sketches and detailed drawings showed his visionary talents. Walking today's path, he would see his visions, from past times, that came to life in new times.

He would see ornate doorways, classic structures, and elaborate building fronts. He would notice triangular pediments in use, those triangular upper parts of the front of a building. Speaking of building fronts, facade is a Renaissance term and concept that very much is at the forefront of current day architecture. Facades or fronts of symmetry around vertical axis structures and Roman type columns are all around in prestigious (and sometimes non-prestigious) buildings. Da Vinci would have an affinity for bank buildings, corporate office buildings, institutional buildings, and structures at colleges and universities.

High ceilings of yesteryear made an appearance much like those in the town palazzos he was used to being around, with details of beams and colors to match. Below that, ornate floors of Italian marble and tile represented carry over, Renaissance styles of the day's architecture.

All of these are examples of his knowledge visualized.

Da Vinci also, when he looked at architecture, was looking at the "story" of the city: when it was built, why it was built, how it was built, what would people like the most, and how it all ended up. That was the case during his times and those questions apply to today's architecture as well. Next time you are in a city, look around for the "story."

Leonardo's vision had become a reality. His output of sketches and engaging and detailed drawings, proved that visionary quality to be true. Da Vinci was a "visualizer."

A much-needed change from overly decorated and used Roman and Gothic Architectural style, Renaissance architects and artists openly promoted new artistic and architectural ideas or values becoming a symbol for expression through art. They carved their own niche by thinking creatively, way ahead of their time. That's almost the definition of today's architecture.

Da Vinci would see his Renaissance architecture, in present day and see how it was influenced by the Roman architecture that he knew, using techniques like ornamentation. In his time, that would lead to a change in forms of structure. It does in current times, as well. Architects introduced building styles which were more symmetric and structured. Structures took the form of their functionality and not just aesthetics alone. He would see that everywhere in current-day architecture: form and function, buildings with purpose.

Renaissance architects designed buildings making sure that the windows captured and allowed for the most amount of sunlight. Streets were built wide enough to reduce the damage from earthquakes, while also obtaining maximum sunlight. The plan was kept symmetrical and repetitive. Symmetrical and repetitive then, symmetrical and repetitive now.

In Leonardo's ideal city design, his drawings show how perfectly he wanted to design this city in line with Renaissance ideals, yet "modern" (in his day) and "rational" in design.

True artistic innovation can be seen in the way he tried to meld architecture and engineering. He made plans to build a network of waterways and canal systems, but that didn't happen. Although none of his buildings were built, the true revolution lies in his drawings that illustrate his modern (urban) planning skills. He would now see the buildings he wished for, in real life. The envisioned waterways would not be as abundant, probably, as that would be the case regardless or dependent on the city landscape and geography that he landed in.

Architecture by da Vinci placed an emphasis on symmetry, proportion, and geometry. This is demonstrated in the architecture of Renaissance times and in particular, the Pre-Renaissance, ancient Roman architecture which da Vinci borrowed from.

Structured arrangements of columns and supports, as well as the use of semicircular arches, and domes, replaced the look of medieval buildings. Much of this style, as well as new styles and applications, would be in full view to da Vinci on his modern times journey.

Renaissance times truly did represent an influence that opened the way for urbanism and even some of today's architecture. Minds like da Vinci's paved the pathway to what we now know as modernism. The contributions made by Leonardo and other Renaissance architects will always be instrumental in what we now see on display in current times.

Architects plan and design, always with an eye to the future. Their true mindset is envisioning what could be. That was da Vinci's mindset then and would be now, as he thought of new ways, new ideas, and new designs after viewing things in current times.

NATURE

Throughout life, this one and the one past, Leonardo combined art and science in much of his work, studies, notes, and sketches. Much of the affinity for science came from his early childhood rearing in an area surrounded by nature. His upbringing in the Vinci countryside provided for a very abundant environment of nature and his origins of interest in geology, botany, and water might be traced back to his fascination with his natural childhood world.

Wikipedia states that "Nature, in the broadest sense, is equivalent to the natural world, physical universe, material world, or material universe." Nature refers to the phenomena of the physical world, collectively, including plants, animals, the landscape, and other features and products of the earth as opposed to humans or human creations.

Da Vinci saw nature all around and deep within all of his surroundings. This observation would continue. Fortunately, in his visit to new times, da Vinci would see weather, organisms, land masses, rocks, trees, streams, and a life of nature that he was familiar with.

Much of da Vinci's artwork was based on nature which in his mind took many forms and served many purposes encompassing many things, consistent with the stated definition.

His natural childhood environment provided him the perfect chance to study the landscapes, countryside, and surrounding area; it also encouraged him to have interest in drawing and sketching all that he saw, which led to painting. He often recalled the exploration of natural phenomena as influential in his ongoing learning and experimentation and detail which led to many of his artistic contributions (with an emphasis on detail). Studying nature like he did led to art.

Da Vinci would rather explore the countryside and all things about nature than study his school books. You can bet that along the way, there were charcoal pencils used to draw, sketch, and note all that he saw. It was during his countryside trips that Leonardo decided that he would be a lifelong learner, always seeking knowledge and experiencing new things, especially as it related to nature. It was this childhood environment and influence that put him in the perfect mindset for his visit to current times.

Bulent Atalay, author of *Math and the Mona Lisa: the Art and Science of Leonardo,* stated,

> *"No self-respecting artist goes around counting tree branches, but Leonardo did. He was a scientist doing art. It was always the patterns he was after. Proportions, patterns, the mathematics behind it."*

It is obvious from his observations, sketches, notes, and painting that Leonardo held the natural world in high esteem.

For a painter to take such a visible, scientific approach towards nature was unusual in Renaissance times. It probably wouldn't be so uncommon in today's times. Leonardo was a painter. His scientific interests and studies were not detached from nature nor detached from painting, for Leonardo was also a scientist.

Renaissance art historian Kenneth Clark puts it best:

> *"The direction of his scientific researches was established by his aesthetic attitudes. He loved certain forms, he wanted to draw them, and while drawing them he began to ask questions, why were they that shape and what were the laws of their growth?"*

Clark went on to say that Leonardo's delight in drawing and painting natural things merged with his scientific urge and insatiable curiosity powering his art.

For Leonardo, rational knowledge was based on the experience of the senses: His role and man's role was to observe nature as attentively and completely as possible.

Da Vinci's sketches of the natural world suggest his love and respect for the works of nature. He showed this often as he was preparing studies for a larger painting or just observing the nature surrounding him.

Here is an individual who loved to study anything and everything around him. This included all things nature. His sketches show his love of drawing oddly shaped nautilus shellfish, water and its flow, and characteristics and spiral forms like hair. (Take a look at the curls of the people in his portraits!)

He would still try to bring nature to art and architecture and further it to invention much like he did when he observed the nautilus shell, which influenced his idea of a spiral staircase. Nautilus shells inspired ancient architects to add spiral flourishes at the tops of Grecian columns. This was an influence of nature. He approached the study of water in the same way. Leonardo had a fascination with the beauty of flowing water. He wanted to understand the ebb and flow of tides, the origins of rivers and oceans and the water cycle, as well as the destroying effects of water in erosion, floods, rain, and storms.

In today's world, just walking around would show Leonardo a trail of bushes, branches, trees, flowers, streams, rivers, water of many forms in nature and in man-made flowing streams, not to mention the whole animalistic side of nature. Fields of flowers, sunrises and sunsets influenced da Vinci's art. In today's times, he would see erosion. He would see stream flow and eddies. Nautilus shells? Not so much, unless he was seaside.

There would be plenty of nature in the city, probably more than Leonardo was used to in Renaissance Florence and Milan. Today he would be pleased and start to connect and combine his natural observations of:

- Fountains
- Pets
- Many species of birds
- Insects, spiders, and snakes
- Rain
- Sun/shade
- Streams/creeks
- Running water—faucets, toilets (that porcelain bowl for human waste—according to da Vinci)
- Potted plants/hanging plants
- Tree varieties
- Transplanted shrubbery and decorative foliage

- Parks
- Flowers
- Urban gardens

Da Vinci would immediately see that highways and high-rises were the dominant backdrop to city life. He would definitely see a need to bring nature back to cities and, in doing so, make them vibrant, purposeful, and resolute places where citizens could be happy.

Today more than half of the world's population lives in urban settings, and that proportion is projected to increase to more than two-thirds by 2050, way beyond the time of da Vinci's visit to present day Earth and probably way beyond da Vinci's comprehension at the time. Given the sights, he could envision hundreds of cities that don't even exist today springing into existence in the near future.

Da Vinci thinking back to vibrant Florence and its workings, would recognize that getting lots of people to live close together would make creative and efficient use of things like energy, water, waste disposal systems, and land. Although da Vinci didn't say it in these words, it is often said that cities are ecosystems of human habitat. His thinking was always that cities shouldn't compete with nature but coexist with it and incorporate it. That was his dream for both Florence and Milan in his time and would be his dream in modern times and the future.

In today's times, non-da Vinci like thinking people still see urbanization as a destructive force that displaces and extinguishes nature. That may have been true in the past—and may continue to be true when cities are unplanned—but urban living and effective urban planning can lead to more efficient use of resources, nature, and all of the land. Optimal designs and the running of cities so that they are no longer competing with nature but are coexisting with it, or even incorporating it, is the goal. In many cases these goals have been met; in some cases we have a ways to go.

Da Vinci would see the need for residential communities built around a mix of open space, parks, places of business, and farms, keeping high-quality housing for citizens and as much green space as possible: bringing the city to nature.

Da Vinci had already shown his passion for urban planning when designing the ideal city. He would want to be involved in any and all city planning of today. He would look forward to injecting an emphasis on the whole natural component being discussed here. He would still study it and still continue to refine artwork and drawings with the detail he would learn.

More than a century ago, the French geographer Élisée Reclus a renowned writer and anarchist, perceptively predicted in his 1895 publication *In The Evolution of Cities*, that people would always need "the dual possibility of gaining access to the delights of the city ...and, at the same time, the freedom that is nourished by nature." Reclus's idea was visionary. Today, thanks to new technologies and a different way of thinking, the urban-rural divide in city planning is closing, which would be much to da Vinci's delight. Da Vinci thought there should be no other way.

Leonardo's innate affinity with nature, that guided and inspired him, would be no different in modern times. He would watch for patterns, symmetry, consistencies, inconsistencies, and other positive influences. He would try to record, mentally or otherwise, all that he saw: every plant, every tree, every branch, every stream, every animal, and every opportunity to incorporate nature into everyday life. He would have plenty to look at in today's world and times. He would be a very satisfied observer and fulfilled from that standpoint.

The effect of the natural environment on his scientific inquiry would serve, then and now, as a base for his observations.

KNOWLEDGE

"It's an inspiration that one person—off on their own, with no feedback, without being told what was right or wrong—that he kept pushing himself, that he found knowledge itself to be the most beautiful thing."

-Bill Gates, on his purchase of Leonardo's *Codex Leicester*, in 1994, for $30.8 million

Leonardo da Vinci was, without a doubt, a knowledge enthusiast.

It is argued that no man has ever studied more subjects or generated more ideas than da Vinci. This only made him quest for even more knowledge. He didn't have, "Get more knowledge," on his to-do list; it was just in his makeup to seek more.

Da Vinci's quest for knowledge was supported by Renaissance times.

One of the Renaissance era's most noted features was the Revival of Learning, an awakening of the mind and a thirst for new knowledge.

With political events forcing changes, the sharing of new ideas in trading, exploration and city environment arose, and the minds, interests, curiosities, and focuses of all men started to erupt and grow wildly. When those of this Renaissance period witnessed this, they realized that those in the past offered great teachings. That is when the Renaissance Revival of Learning really started.

This resulted in many studies of events, a wider spread study of art and literature, and a broadening of what could be to a degree never before known. This sounds almost identical to da Vinci's recipe for life. It sounds like he was one of the first into the Renaissance Revival of Learning pool. He would assimilate this in current times and associate it with also pushing the boundaries of what we know and what we could achieve, almost regardless of the times.

Not only was da Vinci an artist, engineer, and scientist (among many other labels) he was totally devoted to informing, showing, and teaching the people of his time and to further knowledge for the people of the future. Whether he knew it or not, he consciously was contributing to that Revival of Learning. He had no idea how or what that future influence would be. He was about to step right into it.

The underlying nature and understanding of the inner working of things totally consumed him.

Leonardo had a very curious mind with an insatiable desire for knowledge. Again, another underlying principle of his life and his mission.

Part of seeking knowledge is asking questions. (We'll go into that in more depth later.) Leonardo probably thought and hypothesized that if you ask the difficult questions and ask many of them, and if you are not afraid to search for the answers, then all things are possible whether it is now or 500 years in the future. Welcome to the New World, Leonardo.

Sometimes da Vinci would make an observation of something. Combining this with a vivid imagination and a familiar past, he would make it possible to make great strides in the scientific understanding of anything being observed.

"Learning is the only thing the mind never exhausts, never fears, and never regrets," according to da Vinci himself.

He further stated, "The acquisition of knowledge is always of use to the intellect, because it may drive out useless things and retain the good; for nothing can be loved or hated unless it is first known."

Many of the most impactful individuals throughout human history have been men and women with an unbelievable amount of varied interests and talents and they asked many questions over and over. It is because of this very reason that successful people are so successful.

You can rank Leonardo da Vinci at the top of this list. His expertise, pursuits, and accomplishments span multiple disciplines, methods, and mindsets.

This premise comes from the basic tenet of Renaissance humanism that pointed out that humans are limitless in their capacity for development. That concept led to the notion that people should embrace all knowledge and develop their mental and learning capacities as fully as possible. This is where the term Renaissance man comes from, gifted people of that age who sought to develop their abilities in all areas of accomplishment: intellectual, artistic, social, physical, and spiritual. Look up Leonardo da Vinci in any reference guide and you will see his picture next to this concept and definition.

Da Vinci lived and showed that there is significance in developing one's mind beyond a single subject or specialty and studying a broad spectrum of subjects completely unrelated to the initial topic.

Because of da Vinci's intense study of optics, facial movement, and face muscles, da Vinci developed an immense technical ability to paint and created the most distinct feature of the famous Mona Lisa painting. Attribute this to his broad spectrum of study beyond just painting.

He would learn that there were those, in modern times, that figured a specialist approach was better than studying a broad spectrum of subjects. He would have to reconcile that on his visit and maybe show the benefit of his ways.

Da Vinci benefited from his thoughts on thinking. His perspective appeared to be that learning was to expand your human intellect in ways that you never thought possible: learning to expand the overall thinking process and a perspective on the workings of the world.

The famed da Vinci biographer, Vasari, stated that da Vinci had "…such a power of intellect that whatever he turned his mind to, he made himself master of with ease."

Leonardo lived with what could be termed as a paradox of learning. He was never satisfied with just knowing what he knew. He suffered from what is referred to as frustrated knowledge. That is, as much as you find answers to the many questions, regardless of complexity, there is a reality that suggests that there will always be new questions, many with no readily available or obvious answer or solution in sight.

Although Leonardo was a standout, he did learn many things the same way as others did—studio training for his art, trained by the master Verrocchio, conversing with that master and his associates about all that was and was to be learned, and reading all the books he could get his hands on. Many of these classical texts contributed to his learning.

When the Ottomans toppled Constantinople in 1453, many local scholars fled East and landed in Italy, bringing classical texts with them. This fueled humanism and the quest for even more knowledge.

He also learned, as many others did, through going to school (whatever shape or form was available in his time to him) and continuing his education by discussing his interests with learned experts. Much of his training was varied around the arts: painting, sketching, sculpting, and working with the metals—gold, silver, and bronze.

Da Vinci was very sociable and not afraid to seek out other experts in fields he was interested in learning more about. He would do this through conversation and by collecting books. Books weren't as available then but he pursued a collection of them anyway, and did his share of reading when he could. His notebooks are full of references to books that he knew about and the people who authored them in order to discuss more about his varied interests. Once again, we come back to his natural curiosity that drove that pursuit of information that became his storehouse of knowledge.

Today, he would see so many more places to expand his knowledge. Libraries are in abundance, compared to a less book-rich Renaissance time. Technology allows information to be at a fingertip, expanding knowledge at will, quickly and efficiently. Knowledge would approach today's current moniker reference of "having power." Add this to the many other da Vinci traits and he was one powerful visitor, citizen, human being.

CURIOSITY

"The noblest pleasure is the joy of understanding."

-Leonardo da Vinci

Normally, going to the dictionary to understand a da Vinci concept is not the first thing to do, but when it comes to the concept of curiosity, it's like da Vinci authored the definition. Simply put, the definition is a strong desire to know or learn something. That's Leonardo's whole life captured in one sentence, essentially. Sounds like we've said that before. Of course, there is more, but when thinking about his desire of learning, that's what drove him to his pinnacle.

As biographer Walter Isaacson states it, "His genius was just being passionately curious about everything. He wanted to know everything he could know about our universe, including how we fit into it."

From a young age, the talent that drove his success more than any other, was and is (assuming it continues during the visit to today's times) his relentless curiosity. In all that he did, science, art or otherwise, it can be traced back to that singular superior talent and quality. It was so relentless that you will tire relentlessly of associating the word relentless with his curiosity. It was relentless, no doubt.

Not only did he have the urge, but he had the mental capacity to just stare at something for long periods of time, to just sit and think about something or to ask questions about something to satisfy a curiosity. He had the ability to question conventional wisdom and to re-ask questions about questions he had already asked, all part of satisfying curiosity. He had connections at the top of his mind that drove even more questions.

In today's hustle and bustle world, things move at a faster pace. It seems many people are always in a hurry. Would this afford da Vinci opportunities to stare at something for long periods of time to come up with the right questions to satisfy curiosities? That's what he was used to but today's pace of life could change that. He still would be curious but may have to adapt his ways of satisfying his curiosity.

Curiosity is a common characteristic of geniuses, now, in the past, and will be in the future. Curiosity is described in many ways with many definitions (including the one that sounded like da Vinci wrote it) all with common themes. Here are many of those themes that are often referred to when talking about curiosity:

- Insatiable appetite to learn

- A hunger to search for better answers

- Finding ways to propose new possibilities

- Relentless desire to find out how things work

- Asking un-ending "why" and "what if" questions

Do things sound da Vinci familiar yet? They should. Let's continue with more curiosity themes and characteristics:

- Connecting ideas—similar and dissimilar

- Inquisitive thinking, exploration and learning

- Desire to acquire knowledge and learn with the same desire, as a stated mission

- Quest for continuous learning

- Questioning assumptions and conventional wisdom

- The art of knowing; the art of knowing what is not known

- Being inquisitive

- Experiencing daily life in a different way, reflecting on those experiences

- Discovering the unfamiliar in the familiar

There you have it. If you didn't think "da Vinci" with each one of these points, you are missing the characteristic curiosity of da Vinci that propelled him, separated him from the rest, and allowed him to reach the status of genius in all that he did, as well as equips him for a fruitful journey in today's time.

All of these can be expanded on but the important thing here, as da Vinci visits today, is how do all of these traits and driving forces impact his visit, his observations, and the outcomes in whatever form they take? These also make up a good recipe for observation and satisfying curiosity in the future.

He imagined, he asked lots of questions, he learned, and he studied. It was said that he did very ordinary things in an extraordinary and unconventional way. That same curiosity can be a driving force for others and it would, of course, drive the whole visit to current times. For without that curiosity the visit is an idle, ambling, sightseeing adventure—totally un-da Vinci like.

Leonardo da Vinci kept a zealous and fanatical curiosity throughout life, including at the prime of his career. Yes, that almost is the definition of being insatiable.

He once said, "The noblest pleasure is the joy of understanding."

Leonardo's observation and belief that "everything connects" was the basis of much of his work. Making connections between some of the simplest and unrelated things is one of the most crucial creative and critical thinking skills anyone can ever master.

Relating to the curiosity points detailed above:

Today, da Vinci would observe more new things than he ever imagined.

He would get some answers to all the questions asked, come up with some on his own, and the questions that would go unanswered, he would keep on pursuing. That's where the "relentless" description comes in.

No doubt he would propose new possibilities as that's his nature, unlike most other people today and most people during Renaissance time, whether as artists, scientists, engineers, or other.

In today's times, he would have to observe things differently; he would have to see more. That was also the case in Renaissance times, too.

In new times, in a new place, there is lots to comprehend, lots to pursue. Having a fuller understanding of whatever he was interested in or studying would move the curiosity needle to his satisfaction.

There is more to see in today's world. Whether new times in a new world or in a first time visit to a neighboring city during his time, his thinking would automatically be broadened.

Questions and analysis would support his intuition.

Connecting the unconnected is a given, although many things connected today would be viewed as unconnected until he learned more.

Searching when the obvious wasn't present. That's an elementary rule in pursuing curiosities, but not a common practice. Pursuit of the unknown (current times) does this.

Moving ideas from thought to reality separates da Vinci from the rest of Renaissance men. This trip to reality is a true dream in a new time.

Not being influenced by the fact that something hasn't been done before is another rule of curiosity. This influence would be completely absent allowing for total expansion of thought.

One has to have "time" to be curious. Da Vinci said, "Time stays long enough for anyone who will use it."

Also, related to the number of things to be curious about and the time it would take to question everything, da Vinci asked:

"Do you not see how many and how varied are the actions which are performed by men alone? Do you not see how many different kinds of animals there are, and also of trees and plants and flowers? What variety of hilly and level places, of springs, rivers, cities, public and private buildings; of instruments fitted for man's use; of diverse costumes, ornaments and arts?"

By now, in looking around at current times, da Vinci would recognize many mechanisms available to help with satisfying his curiosities. The whole technology and internet angle is at the forefront, but so is the availability of libraries, publications, and other books, not to mention on-air media. Pick any or all or a combination of the curiosity points described above and these mechanisms come to the forefront of satisfying curiosities. Curiosity would and could be satisfied better and more quickly than at any other point in history. If da Vinci was curious back in the day about how things could get better and how curiosities could get satisfied better, he would be about to see that curiosity satisfaction come to life, real life, more quickly and better, in a new time.

It bears repeating that da Vinci, without question, had a very curious mind. He quickly realized that a curious mind can relate, process, and connect ideas more quickly and better. Leonardo's genius qualities and talents were not a result of built-in mental brilliance. They were a product of all of this curiosity, the common themes discussed, and actions he took on his findings. Many people ask the questions and get the answers, but not many take action on what they learn. All of those outcomes and satisfactions would be noted in his notebooks along with a list of more questions and a pathway of action and more answers. His notebooks were a curiosity "gold mine."

His whole attitude of curiosity would pervade throughout his lifetime and certainly during a visit to current times. Of course, in today's times there would be so much more to be curious about; there is so much more to know about and so much more to understand about how we fit into it. Could he be of the same Renaissance genius with all there is to see and be curious about? Probably not, but that wouldn't stop him. Thoughts on limitation didn't stop him during his day, so why should they today?

Da Vinci knew there was a whole world of things worth being curious about. Now, in new times, his challenge would be finding those to prioritize and explore further.

Leonardo da Vinci saw the world as nobody else did due to the choices he made in his interactions with it. He chose to always be aware and attuned: observing, noting, asking questions, studying, making connections, and concluding.

A naturally curious mind takes interest in a wide range of subjects to find these connections. From these, new ideas are sparked and new solutions to everyday problems are devised.

When open and exposed to new ideas, the more likely it is that one will follow the curiosities, and the more one will be able to connect new information and discoveries with what one has experienced and what one already knows.

He chose to live boldly and differently than others during his time. He was never one to settle, especially as it related to learning and satisfying curiosity after curiosity. He knew of this feeling and passion and said it best:

> *"Iron rusts from disuse; stagnant water loses its purity and in cold weather becomes frozen; even so does inaction sap the vigor of the mind. So, we*

must stretch ourselves to the very limits of human possibility. Anything less is a sin against both God and man."

The phrases of unquenchable curiosity and feverishly inventive imagination come to mind and populate many research reports today.

He may call it passionate curiosity but regardless of what he called it, he woke up every day thinking about pursuing what interested him most and knew that by following his interests and pursuits he would accomplish his goal of continuously learning.

The things Leonardo was curious about were probably, then and now, truly endless. He noted many in his notebooks. Chances are he didn't have enough notebooks or enough time, but he sure had the breadth of curiosity. The same would exist walking around today.

Upon further analysis, it can be seen how things blend together. That's exactly what he would watch for today.

Early in his career he was involved in fairs, festivals, and producing theatrical performances, especially for royal and elite audiences. Some of his early inventions were to support the production of such events and shows. Even looking at The Last Supper, it is a narrative scene that has many hints of a theatrical performance tied to it. All of this shows that imagination supported curiosity. Curiosity supported knowledge, and that supported art.

Fundamentally, this was proof that da Vinci was a master at blending fantasy with the real world.

Da Vinci would treat his pursuits as part of living life, not work. No one would be happier in the visit to new times and living life in new times, in the real world, than Leonardo da Vinci. His curiosity would continue to be euphoric for him.

ASKING QUESTIONS

"Judge a man by his questions rather than by his answers."

-Voltaire

Everyone, everywhere asks questions every day. Leonardo da Vinci did, too. Many people of a genius level have reached their status by asking, not just answering, not just having conversations, and not just participating in dialogue. Asking questions in the right way enough times, over and over, eventually shaped them into that state of being a gifted genius.

The real experts then knew they were best guided by their own curiosity. Real experts today are guided by the same. They would ask the right questions first, then pursue a solution. That's how they thought, that's how they worked, that's how they came up with their ideas. That's how they made their connections, in their head or from one idea generator to another.

Questions are powerful in many respects. They can take a pool of information, facts, and observations, like those da Vinci would make of his new world, and create bite size pieces of something more defined, more understandable and more manageable than they were before the questions were asked.

Focus is vital when asking questions. Most have a natural tendency to focus on the wrong things that are disconnected from what they are researching or asking about things that send them in a different direction than where they wanted to go. Asking the right questions can prevent that. Imagine da Vinci plodding along the New World paths without asking the appropriate questions. We already know that wouldn't happen. He would ask many questions, relentlessly. You can hear them forming now: "…why this, what if that, how come…."

There is a solution for staying on the right path and staying on task as it relates to asking questions. Detaching one's self from conventional thinking and assumed solutions can suggest different paths, a more correct path, all by asking questions. The questions help to take reality and drill deep to the parts that really matter to the purpose of one's path. Da Vinci would have many purposes for many paths which would lead to many, many questions to stay on his chosen paths.

Put yourself in a new city, a new location and think of how your mind starts working. You start asking questions, whether silently in your own mind or articulated aloud. You ask what things are, why they are like the way they are (form), how things are used, where certain things are and many times, why that would benefit me as well as what's in it for me. All of this sounds like da Vinci's question-asking script for a visit to new times. After all, it is the same script he used in Renaissance times.

Many of the questions that da Vinci asked during his time and those that he would ask in new times didn't and wouldn't immediately add anything to his works of art, his inventions, or his other ventures, but they would and did add to the richness with which he viewed the world. That fruitfulness would eventually contribute to many parts of his work, including the painting of landscapes in his art, the rivers and valleys that he captured, and the expressions, emotions, and the personalities of his subjects.

At a very young age he realized that there was a whole world of things worth his curiosity, but he also realized he had to search for answers regarding them, according to his interests, passions, and pursuits. Asking questions about those would be instrumental and ongoing for his development.

He wasn't striving for certainty with every question asked. He was being guided by his curiosity. Every question might not get answered directly, but asking many questions can guide one to the core of curiosity and eventually answer the big picture question.

Da Vinci and other Renaissance masters knew that great minds chase this curiosity and end up asking great questions. These questions engage the thought on a very regular, if not daily, basis and reflect life's purpose while eventually influencing the quality of life along the way. Da Vinci was living proof that developing an open, inquisitive frame of mind would broaden one's universe and improve the ability to navigate through that universe, all by asking questions and being very, very curious.

Voltaire said, *"Judge a man by his questions rather than by his answers."*

All of this talk of asking questions is an attempt to not only satisfy curiosities but to acquire knowledge. The acquisition of knowledge and learning is best propelled through questioning.

Brilliant ideas can come out of better questions. If one isn't getting the ideas wanted, more questions need to be asked.

The common theme here is keep asking questions. Leonardo's deep curiosity led him to consider literally thousands of questions, which he recorded in journals along with various notes and sketches. Questions led and will lead to active thinking and quests for learning, whether by da Vinci or others mastering the art of asking questions.

In one of his most popular quotes, Einstein stated that if he had an hour to solve a problem, he would spend the first fifty-five minutes making sure he was asking, then answering the right question.

Leonardo, along these same lines, although earlier in time, once said, learning is the only thing the mind never exhausts, never fears, and never regrets.

Like scientists and learned experts today, Leonardo was always ready to revise his thinking and ask more or different questions, when he felt that new observations, answers, or insights required him to do so. This is what leads to so many ideas and eventual connections by da Vinci or anyone thinking the same.

Yes, da Vinci was curious and yes, he was motivated by what he could conceptualize and develop, but he was more interested in the whole process of exploration and investigation than he was in the end product or final results of his efforts.

To get answers and to obtain the right information needed for whatever his creative goal was at the time, he needed to focus on "getting to a path of inquiry." This is the formulation of questions, related and new questions, while continuing to drill deeper and deeper in thought and analysis.

For da Vinci, asking questions was part of his everyday routine. It does seem to be basic and instinctive, but it should not to be taken for granted. As Leonardo found out, really since he was a young child, there is a lot to learn about how to ask the right questions in the right way to get the answers and information sought. Even as a child he asked questions, whether out loud or to himself during his many hikes, walks, or countryside wanderings.

A curious mind can connect ideas better. Da Vinci lived this and experienced this. His mantra was to maintain an open mind and be willing to learn, unlearn, and relearn, all by asking questions, to get the answers needed.

Curiosity develops into an amazing finding. You can identify findings and connections that will allow you to pursue ideas and concepts further, as a result of asking questions.

Leonardo da Vinci was often described (in this case by Sir Kenneth Clark, British Art Historian), as "undoubtedly the most curious man who ever lived." Asking questions about everything (his curiosities) enriched his day-to-day experiences of the world that he walked in, past and present.

So far, we have discussed this topic mostly as it relates to da Vinci, his curiosities, and questions during his lifespan, up until today's time, up until his visit to a new world in new times. Now that he has been dropped into a city, gotten over the initial shock and overwhelm of all that could be seen, the hustle and bustle, and seeing thousands of new things, more "modern," questions of the time would come forth.

Depending on where he was on the spectrum of observation and gaining new knowledge, he would ask questions today like:

- Are there wars going on?

- What is the economy like?

- What are these things you call companies and how important are they?

- Which are the important companies?

- How do people earn commissions, get hired, get paid for work, and what kind of work do all these people do to get paid?

- How does communication happen with all these people?

- What does entertainment consist of?

- What foods are eaten?

- What are meals and food prep like?

- What clothes and costumes are worn?

- How do we get information?

- How do we share information?

- What is this thing called transportation and how is it different from horse travel?

- What will future cities look like beyond what I have predicted?

- Is there space (outer space) travel?

- What is the most valuable resource?

- ◆ What changes happen in society to make it better?
- ◆ What are the biggest concerns and problems for the average citizen?

This list is very limited compared to what may be conceived by the imagination of da Vinci which, as we are finding out, was really limitless.

Albert Einstein said, "Question everything." It surely could be the same thing said by da Vinci for that is how he lived his life and how he developed his ideas. He would ask questions with a purpose.

The primary inspiration and motivator behind every inventor, thinker, philosopher, and artist throughout history, like da Vinci, has been a sense of wonder and curiosity.

Questions imply wonder, and spending time in finding an answer often leads and should lead to more questions. This in turn, becomes a quest to learn more, adding to his lifelong quest and mission.

Wherever you are on the curiosity spectrum, it's important to realize that curiosity is a characteristic that can be developed and improved—and it should be—as it is the one trait that can lead to questions that can help us overcome obstacles and challenges more easily.

It sounds repetitive but it is worth restating: The trick is to ask the right questions, for they serve as magic buttons to press that unlock powerful answers, that will enable movement forward. Questions create connection and inspire action in many forms. Da Vinci connected and took action from that inspiration then and would do the same, certainly, now.

When da Vinci dug deep he really wasn't thinking about reinventing industries because not that many had existed long enough to reinvent, but he did question and probe and dig deep to unlock new opportunities whether it was art, science, engineering, or any of the other areas he took interest in. For these new outlooks, he knew it would rely on his ability to question deeply, in an imaginative way, in non-conventional ways, with the hopes of new outcomes.

Early on and in ongoing fashion, he realized that great, well-crafted questions push; they push to make one think, to reflect, and to create a connection to something new.

It has been said that curiosity starts with a thought followed by a question, and then is followed by a lot of learning. That's what curiosity is all about.

In da Vinci's mind, it was relentless curiosity—an insatiable hunger to learn, to question, to search for better answers, to articulate his ideas in pictures, sketches, writing, and art, all while proposing new possibilities.

Einstein went on to say,

"The important thing is not to stop questioning. Curiosity has its own reason for existing. One cannot help but be in awe when he contemplates the mysteries of eternity, of life,

*of the marvelous structure of reality. It is enough
if one tries merely to comprehend a little of this
mystery every day."*

Looking in his many notebooks, regardless of the
emphasis on to-do lists and sketches, there are probably
more questions recorded than anything. Questions
satisfy curiosities. We know that by now. Da Vinci
knew this and expounded on the subject himself:

*"I roamed the countryside searching for answers
to things I did not understand. Why shells existed
on the tops of mountains along with the imprints
of coral and plants and seaweed usually found in
the sea. Why the thunder lasts a longer time than
that which causes it, and why immediately on
its creation the lightning becomes visible to the
eye while thunder requires time to travel. How
the various circles of water form around the
spot which has been struck by a stone, and why
a bird sustains itself in the air. These questions
and other strange phenomena engage my thought
throughout my life."*

He imagined, he asked lots of questions, he learned,
and he studied. His thoughts were engaged. That same
curiosity can be a driving force for others and it would,
of course, drive his whole visit to current times.

Author Michael Gelb stated that,

*"All of us come into this world curious. The desire
to learn more is present from the beginning.*

Great minds go on asking confounding questions with the same intensity throughout their lives. Leonardo's childlike sense of wonder and insatiable curiosity, his breadth and depth of interest, and his willingness to question accepted knowledge never abated….and that fueled the wellspring of his genius throughout his adult life."

Pure and simple, Sigmund Freud said of da Vinci that, "he transmuted his passion into inquisitiveness."

Da Vinci followed this with his own thoughts when he said, "The desire to know is natural to good men."

While we do not know the exact question-asking process da Vinci continually went through or the additional questions he asked, other than what was entered into his notebooks, chances are good that there were many, many "What if…..?" questions. It was these that stimulated his thinking, his imagination, his branches of curiosities, all to shake up current thinking and perspectives on its way to new thinking, new ideas, new connections, and new opportunities. Da Vinci had one of the greatest pools of opportunity ever known in history and was one that pursued them vigorously without being clouded. Asking questions played a larger part in that then and now, more than he realized.

Conversation with him, in current times, would consist of more questions than statements (probably on both sides). What do you think?

OBSERVATION

"A mind that can connect the seemingly unconnected can make the most of brain."

-Maria Konnikova, Harvard psychologist
and author of *Mastermind: How
to Think Like Sherlock Holmes*

Da Vinci was obsessed with observation. Observation was his way of paying attention and in his case much attention to detail. He would look at streams of water and describe the swirls and the energy among them. He would look at a seashell and assimilate other similar shapes and functions. His ability to observe was due to his many experiences and breadth of interests.

Most of those observations ended up in notebooks that da Vinci would review, re-read, analyze, and wonder "what if" or "how come?" He looked for patterns within these observations that would then lead to more observation, more questions, more connections, and more ideas.

To make the scientific observations that da Vinci made, it took an aesthetic eye and creative mind working hand in hand. On a trip to a new city in new times he would be the king of observation.

Leonardo relied on his senses for the basis of meaningful experience. He mostly relied on his visual sense, but the others came into play. He discusses the promise of science (or not) in his book, *Treatise on Painting*:

> *"To me it seems that those sciences are vain and full of error which are not born of experience, mother of all certainty, firsthand experience which in its origins, or means, or end has passed through one of the five senses. And if we doubt the certainty of everything which passes through the senses, how much more ought we to doubt things contrary to these senses such as the existence of God or of the soul or similar things over which there is always dispute and contention."*

In encountering today's world, no doubt, Leonardo would have been skillful and bright at visualizing information and extending his observations for others to visually see, much like his painting masterpieces, sketches, notes, and drawings. His visualization would consist of looking at something and comparing it to what he knew and what he was already familiar with, then the whole imagination, question asking, connectivity parts of his psyche would kick in. Secondarily, he would be the king of visualization.

Leonardo was a lateral thinker. He was obsessed in his thinking with seeing its implications and connection for other areas.

By now, it is clear to see primary characteristics of da Vinci's thinking process. It starts with curiosity that leads to observation which then translates into written form into one of his many notebooks. From there he would learn from things and apply the detail learned. Da Vinci always tried to show what he saw. Da Vinci realized these were the vital parts of the creative and thinking process that he lived and practiced every day. These had a major hand in paving the way towards his great discoveries, concepts, ideas, and inventions.

Leonardo observed his surroundings which included other people, animals, landscapes, and nature, and used those observations to add more realism to his paintings. He did this from the details of observation. He noticed then and would notice now how things looked in different light, from different vantage points—more material for notebook entries.

Leonardo's observations of nature in motion directly provided him a base for his ability to portray human movement in the artistic masterpieces for which he is known today.

It was reported from Leonardo's time that he was always pleased whenever he encountered a strange head, face, head of hair, or beard of unusual appearance. He would follow that person for a whole day, observe, and memorize the detail, all so that when he reached home he could draw the subject as if they were present. This power of observation was essential then and would certainly be the crux of a visit to today's world.

Da Vinci is admired for those powers of observation as they blend in with imagination, curiosity, knowledge, and other da Vinci principles. Da Vinci excelled in capturing his observations in his notebooks, whether words or images. Da Vinci was a master at understanding and applying the art of visualizing like no other Renaissance figure and maybe like no other person in modern times. These observations added vigor and vitality to his work, especially his paintings.

Walter Isaacson wrote,

> *"He recorded his observations, looked for patterns among them, and then tested those patterns through additional observation and experimentation. Leonardo da Vinci is the ultimate example of how the ability to make connections across disciplines—arts and sciences, humanities and technology—is a key to innovation, imagination, and genius."*

Da Vinci explains his own power of observation by his quote, "The artist sees what others only catch a glimpse of." This is typical da Vinci and is an example of "deep down" observation. Every phenomenon that he was interested in and pursued further began as close observations followed by thought, hypothesis, experimentation, and finally, practical knowledge to be applied. Da Vinci was not afraid to re-think or to re-theorize if he gained new information and new facts from more observation.

FOCUS

Da Vinci would find that the custom in current times is to focus and not get distracted by many things. In today's times, that distraction is called Shiny Object Syndrome.

Shiny Object Syndrome is a disease of distraction, and it affects people like da Vinci specifically because of the qualities that make them unique. It's called Shiny Object Syndrome because it's the equivalent of a small child chasing after shiny objects every time it sees one.

Many feel that increasing distractions and diversions are weaknesses as a society.

Leonardo understands and lives with the fact that both have value: being focused on things that fascinate and intrigue us and falling into a distraction trap and deciding to pursue some novel new idea (the shiny object) that is stumbled upon. Balancing focus with many interests is something da Vinci would have to achieve when involved with the Internet or any of the many other distractions of today's times, but he could do it well.

Much is written here about many of the soft skills that produced hard output, theoretical concepts, and lots of knowledge. We have discussed curiosity, imagination, knowledge, invention, and more. It is worthy at this point to make a comment related to perspective since it was one inherent trait of the great mind of da Vinci.

Perspective is a way we can see life, situations, the environment, problems, opportunities, and people, from many different views. Perspective helps create the thinking that connections can be made. Perspective comes from new ventures like visiting today's time and comparing it to the familiar past, education, and observation—da Vinci style, culture, conventional wisdom, and the world around a person currently. All that supports the conventional wisdom of perception becoming reality. That was the case for Leonardo; connections galore amongst reality.

Perspective has a Latin root meaning "look through." When talking perspective, it usually has something to do with looking or seeing. Da Vinci always talked about the superior sense of seeing. That supports superior perspectives.

He would go on to discover and experience that a change in perspective leads to more questions and more curiosity. That is the base of new creativity, connections, and concepts.

Michael Michalko, author of *Creative Thinkering: Putting Your Imagination to Work,* talks about da

Vinci consciously thinking about connecting ideas. He stated,

> *"He would gaze at the stains of walls, or ashes of a fire, or the shape of clouds or patterns in mud or in similar places. He would imagine seeing trees, battles, landscapes, figures with lively movements, etc., and then excite his mind by conceptually blending the subjects and events he imagined and his subject. Da Vinci would occasionally throw a paint-filled sponge against the wall and contemplate the random stains and what they might represent."*

Maria Konnikova, a Harvard psychologist and author of *Mastermind: How to Think Like Sherlock Holmes,* says, "A mind that can connect the seemingly unconnected can make the most of brain."

His observations would be over-engaged in new times in a new world.

Da Vinci is admired for his powers of observation. He observed everything. This included nature, people, and the environments he lived and worked in. He visualized connections and what could be with all of this observation. Da Vinci understood the art of visualizing like no other. Guess what he was about to do in his new time-enriched, observation playground environment?

EXPERIMENTATION

As the Renaissance era was ramping up, da Vinci was doing more and more for his knowledge and craft. Much of his efforts centered around experimentation.

Science, as we know it today as a method of experimentation, observation, and the gaining of knowledge, did not exist in early Renaissance times. Required scientific knowledge of natural phenomena was mostly from the writings and teachings of ancient Greeks like Aristotle and other philosophers of pre-Renaissance times. This information was presented by theologians and the Church, while condemning scientific experimentation. While greatly influenced by the writings of these ancient Greeks and Romans, Leonardo went against conventional thinking, saw the limitations of seeking the truth solely in those writings or the Bible, and decided to go the way of observation and experimentation.

In his own words, this was his take on experimentation: "First I shall do some experiments before I proceed farther, because my intention is to cite experience first and then with reasoning show why such experience is bound to operate in such a way. And this is the true rule by which those who speculate about the effects of nature must proceed." Chalk that up to Renaissance thinking and the times.

Leonardo's work linked some of the unscientific methods of his time with much of today's modern approach of experimentation and experience-based observation.

Leonardo single-handedly developed a new scientific approach, involving the observation of nature and its surroundings, conceiving and asking questions along with reasoning and mathematics. Call it what you want, but most today would label it as the scientific method.

In da Vinci-like thinking, Leonardo's quest for knowledge and understanding meant connecting it with other phenomena and experiences through a similarity of patterns. For example, when he studied the proportions of the human body, he compared them to the proportions of buildings in Renaissance architecture. His research and study of muscles, bones, and other parts of the human anatomy, led him to study and draw gears, moving parts and levers, as a link from anatomy to engineering. Da Vinci loved water and the study of it. Patterns of water flow led him to observe similar patterns in the flow of air and from there led to more and more connections of nature.

This ability to connect observations and ideas from different areas of study is the base of Leonardo's approach to learning and research. Making connections like these in today's time would depend on his familiarity, brought forward, to present form, with expanded patterns and connectivity.

Leonardo used this method of scientific inquiry as much as he could. That method consisted of close observation, repeated testing of that observation, realistic illustration of the subject observed or the phenomenon in play, with explanatory notes to support his observations. The result was volumes of remarkable notes on a variety of topics, from the nature of the sun, moon, and stars to the formation of fossils and, perhaps most notably, the mysteries of flight.

Leonardo was very sensory, relying much on his senses to guide him through experiences. For Leonardo, his emphasis on the senses was mainly visual. Today it goes way beyond that, backed by research and access to information and computers. However, confronted with all that is going on in today's world, Leonardo would have been brilliant at visualizing the information available.

Through the power of observation, he was able to grasp the significance of complex phenomena and the relationships between variables. This carried through to all of his work, with or without the approval of non-humanist minded citizens.

IMAGINATION

"Why does the eye see a thing more clearly in dreams than the imagination when awake?"

-Leonardo da Vinci

In all that is talked about here, there are a number of continuous themes: new ideas, knowledge, interests, curiosities, and way, way more. Visualizing many related things to these that can't be seen, especially at their origination, and bringing them to real things is the very definition of imagination. Da Vinci wouldn't state that as a definition but he surely would portray it, live out its meaning, and experience it daily. That is really what da Vinci was thinking when he pondered, "Why does the eye see a thing more clearly in dreams than the imagination when awake?"

The Stanford Encyclopedia of Philosophy states:

"To imagine is to represent without aiming at things as they actually, presently, and subjectively are. One can use imagination to represent possibilities other than the actual, to represent times other than the present, and to represent perspectives other than one's own. Unlike perceiving and believing, imagining something does not require one to consider that something to be the case."

"Endless possibilities" was something Leonardo learned in his early family life. His mother provided him a sense of "no boundaries," a limitless world, more than just the family unit of his small Italian town of Anchiano, near Vinci. From this, both he and she saw endless possibilities. What direction that teaching would take was not known yet, but off it went like a modern-day rocket.

The reason this is all important to da Vinci is that imagination plays a role in the acquisition of knowledge. Call it curiosity, call it questioning, or call it thinking, it all is related to gaining more and more and more knowledge along an unending path.

In present day, he would "visualize" many things that couldn't be immediately seen or even thought of yet. They would generate question after question after question as that was his basis for satisfying curiosities, making connections and bringing new things to reality, at least in his wandering mind. He would explore "what could be"? Imagination at work.

For da Vinci, this is his power of creativity. It is often said that someone had a great imagination to come up with a particular idea. The corollary exists as well, for those without new ideas are referred to as having no imagination.

It is said that da Vinci studied, observed, and visualized things with his whole brain: both the right side and the left side. It is that whole brain thinking that allowed him to combine ideas and that fed his imagination. He applied what is now termed right-brain thinking, also known as the creative side: art, creativity, imagination, intuition, hypothetical thinking, and the asking of questions, and left-brain thinking that is referred to as the analytical side: mathematics, science, logic, analysis, linear thinking and more. Whole brain thinking allowed for the connections between unrelated things which propels imagination to the highest levels.

A high level of imagination fuels invention. In combining thoughts, both sides of the brain, and connections of ideas, he urged those he worked with and taught to look at how they could relate, even though un-relatable at the start. (See the imagination definition.) Looking off in the distance at mountains, the sky, clouds, the ground, trees, and thinking of whole landscapes, villages, and environments was a small, small example of things to fuel the imaginative mind.

Looking at rocks, swirling water, and underwater life, blending and comparing was another combination at work, more imagination to the forefront. From here, new painting backdrops could evolve, new thoughts on underwater life, working mechanisms, alive or not. These were all just the tip of the imagination artwork at work using whole brain thinking.

Michael Gelb, author of *How to Think Like Leonardo da Vinci* states that this represents a breakthrough in the evolution of human thought, while giving birth to thinking that resulted in the modern day concept of brainstorming. In brainstorming there are no rules, much like imagination resulting from having no biases or ceilings of thought.

Simply seeing things differently, without conventional influences and preconceptions, positioned Leonardo da Vinci far ahead of his time. Stepping foot in present day would surely eliminate conventional influences and preconceived notions.

Thinking and dreaming big, with creativity and imagination at work, involves reaching beyond what is commonly known by other people. It's about thinking from the future back, rather than from here to the future. This unlocks boundless possibilities for creativity for finding the very best potential, with no ceilings and with no biases. Leonardo da Vinci lived in a world and now stepping forward, where he thinks big before he starts thinking small, establishing a sound base for creativity.

According to Michael Michalko, a highly-acclaimed creativity expert and author, "The metaphors that Leonardo formed by forcing connections between two totally unrelated subjects moved his imagination with a vengeance."

His mind was an extraordinary playground where ideas from nature and beyond intermingled with his own inspiration.

So what does all this mean as da Vinci steps foot on today's planet Earth and how is imagination at play?

One of the key things, just stated, is that imagination plays a role in the acquisition of knowledge.

Looking around at the cityscape, the environment, nature, and all surroundings, da Vinci would start to connect. He would start to combine ideas and freshly observed concepts.

He would play a game of what ifs; he would start listing (in his notebooks or his mind) questions related to cross concepts and combining thoughts (right brain, left brain, whole brain).

As da Vinci viewed all around him in present day he would brainstorm his observations by combining unrelated thoughts, ideas, and concepts in full view to come up with new thinking and new potential realities.

I'm not da Vinci, but here are potential examples of those thoughts as he landed in today's time, thinking in terms of "what if," "what could be," "how would," questions:

WARNING: these are far-fetched much like da Vinci's contemporaries thought about his ideas, much like any set of brainstorming ideas but think about what happens when cross pollinating ideas/concepts.

- A windowless building; a building with glassless windows.

- Swings hung from something overhead to move from one building to another

- Painted murals decorating streets, sidewalks, and buildings

- Confined sleep pods for short duration sleep in public

- Incorporation of all animals in urban environments paying attention to waste, nourishment, and more.

- Underwater travel, underwater cities

- Robotic butlering

- Using the power of wind to generate electricity, to make cars go, and to power other horseless carriages and vehicles

- Plant life healing small wounds and famine

- Foods/meals that last a long time reducing eating frequency

- Psychological predictions: knowing problems, thoughts before they

become real and having a solution
before they are problems

- Brain recorders

- Addressing instant virtual thought
  with real instant information

- Garments to hold charge and emit
  charge for technological devices

- Not being tied to video screens—seeing
  graphics on wall displays, holographic
  displays, displays on your body

- Virtual cleaning: walking through
  something to be instantly cleaned
  and free of disease, probably while
  also getting a health assessment

These ideas and examples are crude, brainstormed examples but lend themselves to his present-day state of mind and thinking and would carry him on his way in his journey here (500+ years later).

The ability of Leonardo's transdisciplinary thinking in combining different areas and solving complex problems will be the great intellectual and professional asset of new generations, even after da Vinci's visit to new times.

EPILOGUE

"Leonardo da Vinci was a man of regal spirit and tremendous breadth of mind; and his name became so famous that not only was he esteemed during his lifetime, but his reputation endured and became even greater after his death."

-Giorgio Vasari

Now that da Vinci has seen the New World, new technology, new ideas, etc. and now that he has combined, cross-connected, and joined like concepts, what would he come up with for future visits by others 500 years into the new future? What ideas would represent the next cultural, technical, scientific and intellectual explosion? After all, listening to history to see into the future is what we set out believing and stating.

During your reading time with this book, we've been discussing the mind of Leonardo da Vinci and the intellectual qualities that helped make him one of the greatest innovators of all time.

By now you know da Vinci was more than a painter, more than a scientist, more than an inventor, and more than an engineer. He is the symbol of a broader more fulfilling, intelligent, and expansive way of thinking and doing. He represented a multidisciplinary way of thinking. In today's times, we are in need of more of this. Maybe reading how his observances created new perspectives and eventually new solutions will be a primary take away from this book for you.

As I hope you will agree by now, Leonardo was a Renaissance man. I hope you now know what a Renaissance man is and how he thinks. He was more than all those things listed above. He was a genius. I'm proud to call him that. He deserved that title. Whether it is from his times or present day, who else comes to mind with the breadth of observation, curiosity, knowledge, and application as da Vinci does? The answer is probably no one or, on a stretch basis, maybe one or two people.

When it comes to connecting art, science, and design, no one did it better than Leonardo da Vinci. I hope you were inspired by what you just read. Many of his lessons, teachings, and ideas can be connected to more than art, science, and design. That is up to you to make those connections, as he did and you will. Go ahead; ask more questions.

Da Vinci wasn't superhuman. He had his faults. He was a procrastinator, ignored deadlines, left projects uncompleted, and more. He overcame all of this with his perspectives and eventual contributions.

One of the things to leave with here, forgetting curiosity, observance, knowledge, and intellect is that da Vinci enjoyed conceiving ideas more than he did completing them.

Unending has been a term applied to much of his learning. Think about his insatiable appetite for curiosity, the asking of question after question, his observance for potential connections. He lived his life with these at the forefront, start to finish. Start to finish suggests a long and winding venture and journey. For Da Vinci that was relentless. Leonardo applied his intellect. He thought differently. He saw breakthroughs and connections no one else saw. That's what made him different. That's what made him perfect for a visit to today's time, 500 plus years after his death. This all influenced many after his demise and will continue to do that well into the future.

I hope as you reflect on this writing, you are inspired to become as well-rounded, as creative, and one with application as you continue to be the best version of yourself that you can be.

Here are your lessons to help you on your way to being da Vinci like:

- ♦ Have unending curiosity about everything

- Learn, learn and learn—by experimentation, observation, and from others
- Have no rules for imagination, wonderment, or connecting ideas
- Visualize ideas
- Think about what hasn't been researched or discovered
- Ignore conventional wisdom
- Chase ideas, dreams, passions, and "what ifs"
- If you don't like the outcome, revisit it
- Organize information
- Fuel creativity
- Never say it can't be done or proven

Undeniably, Leonardo accomplished more than any other human being could possibly dream of in a lifespan, but one wonders what would have been the impact of his work on history if he had effectively published and circulated his intuitions, ideas, concepts, and discoveries.

Besides the beauty of his art and the mesmerizing power of his observations, Leonardo da Vinci should also be remembered for his extraordinary wandering mind, his dedication to learning, and exploring the wonders of human life and nature.

Giorgio Vasari said of him, "Leonardo da Vinci was a man of regal spirit and tremendous breadth of mind; and his name became so famous that not only was he esteemed during his lifetime, but his reputation endured and became even greater after his death."

Leonardo's remains lie in a chapel in Amboise. As for Mona Lisa, she survived a revolution and two world wars after Leonardo brought her to France over 500 years ago. He continued to work on her right up until his death.

And finally, I leave you with this from a featured article in *The Saturday Evening Post* about Life Lessons Learned from da Vinci:

> *"There is no reason you actually need to know any of this. It is information that has no real utility for your life, just as it had none for Leonardo. But maybe you, like Leonardo, want to know. Just out of curiosity. Pure curiosity."*

Stay curious!

ACKNOWLEDGMENTS

Forgive me for being emotional, choked up, and a bit sappy here, but this is truly a heartfelt feeling of thanks and that is to the one by my side on life's journey who is more than a best friend: my wife Julie Ann. She is my number one cheerleader, motivator, and supporter in not only this labor of love, but in anything I do. The best ventures though, are the ones we do together, like the trip to Florence, Italy to do research for this book. This is a big acknowledgment for her and her love. I love you, Julie Ann.

Daughter Allison continues to be right behind her as a fan. To see what she does that reminds me of me, is ever satisfying. She was with me during most of the writing of this book and it was a joy having her around during that time. Glad she is enjoying the big leagues and living her dream! Thanks Gator. I love you.

Behind the scenes, but still with words of encouragement are Courtney, Bradley, Caden, and Carsen. They don't always voice their support but they let it be known in other ways. They are an important part of my life and ones also in the forefront of my mind.

To assemble a project like this takes a team. The two leaders that I acknowledge big thanks to are Barbara Grassey and Stephanie Chandler. Both know the book publishing business better than most and their advice and suggestions were invaluable; Barbara is an editor and advisor extraordinaire and Stephanie is one of the most resourceful in the business. It was her resources that put the finishing touches on this to bring it to fruition. Cathi Stevenson and Gwen Gades have offered phenomenal assistance in creating the cover design and in producing this book. A big thank you to them for making my vision even more real.

Family and friends all play an important role in all that I do. I am very, very grateful and thank each and every one of them.

Last, but certainly not least, and it feels kind of funny to do this, but I'm going to do it anyway, and that is offering thanks to Leonardo da Vinci. He has offered more than expected and taking this journey with him made me feel like I was right by his side the whole way. His lessons, teachings, methods, and philosophies are something to learn from on the way to being a better person. Thank you Master!

And then there's Lu, and this time around, NOLA and Ivy.

-Al Lautenslager

BIBLIOGRAPHY AND SOURCING

Atalay, Bulent. Math and the Mona Lisa: The Art and Science of Leonardo. Smithsonian Books, 2004.

Back to the Future. Directed by Robert Zemeckis. Universal Pictures, 1985.

Brown, Dan. *The Da Vinci Code.* Doubleday, 2003.

Gelb, Michael. *How to Think Like Leonardo Da Vinci.* Random House Publications, 1998.

Civilisation: A Personal View by Kenneth Clark. Directed by Michael Gill. BBC Television Documentary, 1969.

Decoding da Vinci. Directed by Doug Hamilton. PBS. 2019.

Isaacson, Walter. *Leonardo da Vinci—The Biography.* Simon & Schuster, 2017.

ItalianRenaissance.org

Konnikova, Maria. *Mastermind: How to Think Like Sherlock Holmes*. Penguin Books 2013

Lester, Toby. *Da Vinci's Ghost: Genius, Obsession, and How Leonardo Created the World in His Own Image. Free Press, 2012.*

Michalko, Michael. *Creative Thinkering: Putting Your Imagination to Work*. New World Libraries, 2011.

The Stanford Encyclopedia of Philosophy. Plato.stanford.edu

Vasari, Giorgio. *Lives of the Most Excellent Painters, Sculptors, and Architects*. 1550.

Wikipedia.com. Various entries.

Abrahams, Dr. Peter. Professor of Clinical Anatomy at Warwick Medical School, England, Visiting Professor, Anatomy Faculty, St. George's University.

Alberti, Leon Battista. Italian Humanist, Architect, Principal Initiator - Renaissance Art Theory. (1404-1472).

Arouet, Francois-Marie aka Voltaire. French Enlightenment writer, historian, philosopher. (1694-1778).

Finkers, Herman. Dutch cabaret artist. (1954-)

Gross, Dr. Karen. Contributor, *Huffington*

Post; Former President, Southern Vermont College; Former Senior Policy Advisor, US Department of Education.

Porrini, Sergio. ItaliaLiving.com contributor.

Reclus, Élisée. Renowned French geographer, writer and anarchist. (1830-1905)

Syson, Luke. Art historian, Head of Fitzwilliam Museum in Cambridge, Chairman of European Sculpture and Decorative Arts at New York's Metropolitan Museum of Art.

Santayana, George. Philosopher, essayist, poet, and novelist. (1863-1952)

Verdon, Monsignor Timothy. Art historian, Art teacher in Florence; Stanford University; Canon of the Florence Cathedral. (1946-).

Made in the USA
Monee, IL
18 June 2020

32976285R00156